the FLY-TYING
BIBLE

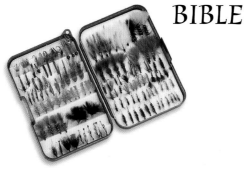

the FLY-TYING
BIBLE

100 deadly trout
and salmon flies in
step-by-step photographs

Peter Gathercole

A QUARTO BOOK

First edition for the United States, its territories and dependencies,
and Canada published in 2003 by Barron's Educational Series, Inc.

All inquiries should be addressed to:
Barron's Educational Series, Inc.
250 Wireless Boulevard
Hauppauge, New York 11788
http://www.barronseduc.com

International Standard Book No. 0-7641-5550-4

Library of Congress Catalog Card No. 2002109917

QUAR.FLYB

Conceived, designed, and produced by
Quarto Publishing plc
The Old Brewery
6 Blundell Street
London N7 9BH

Editor Paula Regan
Senior art editor Penny Cobb
Designer Penny Dawes
Text editors Claire Waite, Alice Tyler
Photographer Peter Gathercole
Illustrator Christopher Jory
Indexer Pamela Ellis

Art director Moira Clinch
Publisher Piers Spence

Manufactured by Universal Graphics, Singapore
Printed by Midas Printing Ltd, China

9 8 7 6 5 4

Contents

Introduction

There is something almost magical about catching a fish on an artificial fly. Casting to a trout that has been spotted feeding, seeing the fly drift gently into its path, then watching it being sipped down as if it were a real insect, produces a mixture of anticipation and excitement that never dulls. The only thing that could possibly make the thrill even better is if you had created the fly yourself.

Although it is possible to buy any number of effective fly patterns, the ability to tie flies adds another dimension to an already absorbing pastime. It has a practical side, too, making sure that the fly box remains plentifully supplied at all times. Most importantly, though, it gives the fly-fisher the opportunity to take part in the development of fly-fishing itself. Many of the best fly patterns in use today were created by practical anglers who had an idea to create a fly that would be more effective than any pattern they already knew. Patterns like the Muddler Minnow, the Adams, and the Royal Wulff are now all part of established fly-fishing lore, but at one time they were new and revolutionary, created by anglers with a specific problem to solve. With the ability to tie flies, and with it the understanding of what goes into making a fly successful, any angler has the opportunity to take his place in fly-fishing's continuing development.

The ability to tie flies ensures that the fly box is always plentifully supplied.

Catching fish on artificial flies has a long and distinguished history. It is said that the ancient Greeks were the first to catch trout on a fly some 2,000 years ago, from the river Aestraeus. What they created by wrapping red wool and brown cock hackles around a hook has much in common with some fly patterns still in use today. Over the millennia, the range of flies has been expanded and improved so that present-day fly-fishers

have a vast number of patterns at their disposal, tied to imitate anything from a midge to a baitfish.

What makes fly-fishing so popular is the sheer number of species that can be caught. Along with the accepted game-fish species—such as trout and salmon —grayling, char, and even a variety of saltwater fish can all be taken on an artificial fly. Because of this diversity of species and water types, the number of fly patterns in use today is almost impossible to count. Where once there were just two types of flies—those that floated and those that sank—today there are a variety of fly classifications, divided into five main groups that describe, in general terms, what each individual fly is designed to imitate and how it is to be fished.

Dry-fly fishing for Cutthroat trout on the Snake River at Jackson Hole.

Dry flies, as the name suggests, are intended to be fished on the water's surface, and are often tied to imitate the adult stage of one of the many aquatic insect species. Many are tied with special water-resistant materials or treated with a chemical flotant to help prevent them from absorbing water.

Nymphs and bugs feature imitations of the various larvae and pupae of aquatic insects plus a number of crustaceans. Because these particular invertebrates live underwater, their imitations are tied to sink rather than float and often incorporate some form of weight in their dressing.

7

Wet flies are more impressionistic
in their construction than many other
fly types, using mostly natural furs
and feathers to suggest a particular insect
rather than being intended as a close copy.
Hairwings and Streamers make up the fourth and
fifth groups. Both actually fulfill a very similar purpose,
and are either tied merely to stimulate the fish's
inquisitiveness or to imitate one of the various species of
baitfish. What separates them is the material from which
they are made. Hairwings, not surprisingly, have a wing
fashioned from hair, such as bucktail or squirrel tail, while a streamer's wing
is comprised of some form of feather, such as cock hackles or marabou.

Artificial trout and salmon flies come in an incredible range of sizes, colors, and forms.

Even though many flies look very different from one another, most
employ similar techniques in their construction. These techniques are the
building blocks of the craft and must be learned before tyers can create flies
of their own.

The Fly-tying Bible takes the tyer through all of the major fly types in use
today. By showing how to create 100 of the most effective fly patterns in
clear step-by-step photography, the following pages will give the reader a
thorough grounding in all the techniques, encompassing basic to advanced
fly-tying. Using patterns ranging from the simplest winged dry fly through
wet flies and streamers, right up to true-to-life stonefly nymph and baitfish
imitations, this book offers a practical way to master the relevant methods
needed to fill the fly box with proven fish-catching patterns.

If you have not considered tying your own flies, assuming perhaps that it
is an art to which you could never aspire, then think again. For while there
are artistic elements to fly-tying, it is, in reality, a craft that anyone can
learn. All you need is patience, practice, and the right instruction.

How to use this book

This book is divided into five sections: dry flies, nymphs and bugs, wet flies, streamers, and hairwings. Each finished fly is photographed and annotated to show the materials it is tyed with—this can be used as an "ingredients list" before you start. The step-by-step photographs and written instructions take you through the process in clear detail from beginning to end, and additional information tells you which fish species can be caught with each fly.

Introduction:
This introduction to the fly includes information on its individual features, hints and tips for tying the pattern, and suggested color and size variations

Step-by-step photographs:
Step-by-step color photographs illustrate the tying of the fly at every stage

Fish species:
You'll find the species of fish that can be caught with each fly listed here

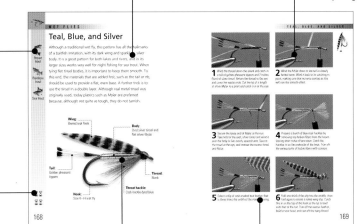

Degree of difficulty:
Rated on a scale of one to five, with one being the simplest, these icons display the degree of difficulty involved in tying each fly

Finished fly:
A photograph of the finished fly is annotated to show the materials used for each part of the pattern

Written instructions:
Clear, expert instruction guides you through each stage—from fixing the hook in the vise, to casting off the tying thread

9

Basic Techniques

There are a number of basic techniques common to the majority of fly patterns, primarily the methods used for starting and finishing a fly. Casting a fly can be tough on the materials secured around the hook, and many game fish are equipped with enough teeth to do a fly a great deal of damage when they actually take. For this reason, it is important to know how to start a fly off properly and, more importantly, how to finish it so that it stays in one piece. There is little point in going to all the trouble of creating an elaborate and beautifully tied fly for it to unravel after only a few

A fine brown trout, which took a deep-fished nymph, about to be returned.

casts. Therefore, the stronger and more secure it can be made in the first instance, the better.

Unless otherwise stated, always begin a fly with tight, close turns of tying thread to build a solid base onto which the various materials can be secured. Then, when all the materials have been added and your creation is sitting proudly in the vise, complete it with a strong, secure whip finish. That way your fly is sure to catch you plenty of fish before it needs discarding.

In the following sequences, a large hook and thick thread have been used to help illustrate the techniques.

It is essential that your finished fly not only looks beautiful, but is also strong and robust.

▼ Fixing the hook in the vise

The hook must be held firmly and securely before you begin tying. In the past, tyers used their fingers to hold the hook, but today it is recognized that using a specially designed vise is by far the best method of achieving the necessary stability.

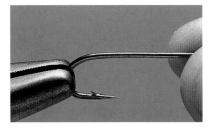

1 Adjust the vise so that the gap between the jaws is slightly greater than the thickness of the hook.

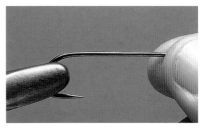

2 Slip the hook bend into the jaws, holding the hook so that the shank is perfectly horizontal.

11

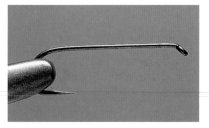 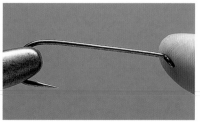

3 Tighten the vise jaws around the hook. If you are using a vise with a lever-action, push the lever down firmly.

4 Check that the hook is held firmly by lightly depressing it. If it can still be moved up and down slightly, then the jaws require further tightening.

▶ Attaching the tying thread

When tying most flies, the tying thread not only binds the materials onto the hook, it also forms a solid base for those materials. Smooth metal hooks don't offer a lot of grip, so to stop the dressing from sliding along the shank, close thread turns are first applied. The thread is usually run on just behind the eye, then wound in close turns along the hook shank. The thread itself is normally fed from its spool using a purpose-designed bobbin holder.

The thread color is usually chosen to match the main body of the fly. However, it is sometimes chosen to contrast and stand out if it is being used to tie a bright head or thorax.

The color of the tying thread is usually chosen to match the body of the fly.

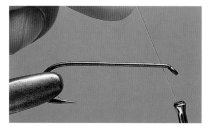

1 With the hook in the vise, hold the tying thread on the far side of the hook with the loose end above the shank and the bobbin holder below.

2 Holding the loose end tight, bring the bobbin holder in front of and above the shank to form a V-shape.

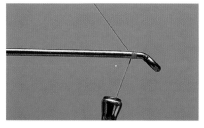

3 While still holding the loose end of the thread upright and tight, begin to wind the bobbin holder end of the thread down the shank.

4 As the thread is wound down the shank, it will begin to cover the loose end, locking it in place.

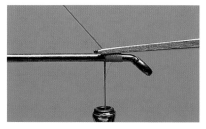

5 After five or six turns of thread have been made, the loose end of the thread will be secure. Put the bobbin holder down and trim the waste end of the thread.

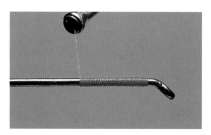

6 Continue winding the thread down the shank, feeding it from its spool with the bobbin holder. Close turns will form the required base.

13

▶ Whip finish

Once the fly is complete, it is important that the thread is cast off properly. The whip finish is a secure method for finishing off a fly. It involves forming a series of slipping loops that are pulled tight over the loose end of the thread, locking it in place. On very small flies, a three-turn whip finish is usually adequate, but on larger patterns, especially where thick threads—above 6/0—are used, five turns give a more secure finish.

It is possible to produce a whip finish with the fingers alone, but many tyers use a specially designed tool called a whip-finish tool (*see page 25*). The tying thread is positioned over the tool's hook and the loop is then wound perfectly around the fly hook.

A whip-finish tool has been used in the following sequence and, to help clarify the technique, no materials have been added to the hook. A thick, more visible thread has also been used. It is useful to note that in normal circumstances, the head of the fly would have already been formed at this stage.

A firm whip finish ensures that the fly is securely tied and able to be reused.

1 With the tying thread positioned just behind the eye, feed a short length of the thread off the bobbin. Hold the thread tight and place the front hook of the whip-finish tool over it.

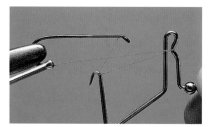

2 Feed more thread from the spool and pass it around the back of the whip-finish tool's arm. Loop the thread around the arm and carry it back in a line parallel to the hook shank to form an inverted figure four.

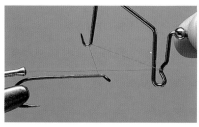

3 Retaining tension on the thread at all times, flip the tool over so that both it and the loose end of the thread are above the hook to form an upright figure four.

4 Rotate the whip-finish tool. The first couple of turns are the most important, as these hold the loose end of the tying thread against the hook. Five turns are normally made, but one or two more are perfectly acceptable.

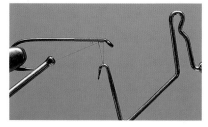

5 Once the required number of turns has been made, the loop must be drawn tight. Carefully flip the thread off the rear arm, retaining tension with the front hook. Pulling the bobbin end of the thread closes the loop.

6 Continue pulling the bobbin end of the thread until the loop is almost closed and the tool's hook is tight against the hook shank. Remove the hook and pull the thread tight. The loose end can now be removed.

▶ Forming the head

The base for a head is added before the whip finish, and is created by adding repeated turns of tying thread to build a neat, slightly tapered profile. Once the whip finish has been made, coats of lacquer are added to the turns of thread, both to protect them and to form a shiny, aesthetically pleasing finish to the fly.

A neat head is formed using tying thread and lacquer.

Various colors of lacquer can be used, depending on the required effect. On a few Atlantic salmon patterns, red lacquer is used, but the more usual colors are black or clear. Clear is the most commonly used lacquer because it allows the color of the tying thread to shine through and can be added to any pattern without the risk of discoloring the materials closest to the head.

Lacquer is normally applied to the head in one to three coats. The more coats used, the shinier the effect. While this is fine for larger flies and streamers, for small flies and nymphs it is inappropriate. Between each coat, the fly can be removed from the vise and left to dry on a rack or a piece of foam. In this way, a number of heads can be completed at one time. The type of lacquer used depends on the finish required: a thin, clear lacquer is perfect for smaller flies while a more viscous product, which dries very hard, works better on larger patterns.

1 Complete the dressing for the fly, adding the body, hackle, wing, etc. Use the tying thread to cover the roots of the wing and build up a neat, smooth, slightly tapered profile. Cast off the thread with a whip finish.

2 Take a drop of clear lacquer on the tip of a dubbing needle and apply it carefully to the head. Always apply lacquer in small drops—if you use too much it will run. Allow the lacquer to soak well into the thread turns, then leave it to dry.

3 Use the point of a dubbing needle to apply black lacquer to the head. Make sure that the colored lacquer does not bleed into the surrounding materials. Allow to dry.

4 Once again, use the point of a dubbing needle to add clear lacquer to make the third coat, making sure that the lacquer is spread evenly over the head.

5 Before the head dries, run a short length of nylon monofilament through the eye. This ensures that the eye remains unblocked and means that the fly can be tied on easily when waterside.

6 Remove the fly from the vise and leave to dry overnight.

17

BASIC TECHNIQUES

▶ Dubbing

Dubbing is the application of fur to the tying thread and a
technique used on a huge number of fly patterns in all of the
major groups. The yarn that dubbing creates is then wound over
the hook shank to form the body or thorax of the fly. What
governs the thickness of the finished body is the amount of fur
added in the first place. Interestingly, applying the fur very thinly,
such as when tying very small nymphs and spider patterns, is the
most difficult method. The temptation is to apply too much fur
creating a body that is thicker than necessary.

The finer the fur, the easier it is to grip onto the tying thread.
Getting coarse furs to stick can be a problem, but there are two
ways to help alleviate this. The first is to apply a thin coat of
beeswax to the tying thread before offering the fur up to it. The
wax acts as an adhesive, though the application should always
be sparing as too much can cause the dubbing fibers to clog.
The second is to make sure that the direction of the dubbing
fiber is well mixed so that the fibers mesh together and are less
likely to fall in line with the thread. If the fur you are using does
appear unidirectional, rubbing a pinch of it in the palm of your
hand should remedy the problem.

The furs and dubbing blends used range from natural furs,
such as seal, rabbit, and muskrat, to man-made products like
Antron and polypropylene. The amount of fur used depends on
the type of pattern and, to some extent, the personal style of
the tyer. Until you have enough experience, it is advisable to
apply the fur in smaller amounts than is necessary. It is always
easier to add more than to remove any excess.

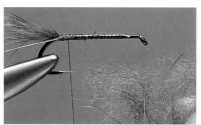

1 With the tying thread positioned to the rear of the hook, and with any tail and ribbing materials already added, apply a thin coat of beeswax to the thread.

2 Take a small pinch of fur, in this case muskrat, enough to cover the tip of one finger. Tease it out slightly.

3 Offer the fur up to the tying thread and spread it thinly along a short length. Make sure the spread is even and that there are no thick spots.

4 Begin to twist the fur between finger and thumb. As you do so, the fur will begin to compact, at the same time gripping onto the thread. Always twist in the same direction, otherwise the fur will not adhere to the thread.

5 Continue twisting, creating as you do so the required yarn. Try to achieve a slight taper to the rear of the yarn, the end nearest the hook, so that the finished body will increase in thickness toward the front end.

6 Wind the dubbing in close turns so that it covers the hook shank. If the pattern has a wing, stop well back from the eye to allow space for the other materials to be added.

▶ Winging loop

When tying in a winging material, whether feather or hair, it is important that the finished wing sits straight and directly on top of the hook shank, to ensure that the fly swims straight when it is pulled through the water. However, there is a tendency for the wing to twist around the hook as it is being tied in, caused by the dragging action of winding the thread. Although a problem with all winging materials, feather wing slips are the most prone to twisting out of position, and they can also split.

The winging loop is the technique used to alleviate this problem. A loose turn of thread is wound over the wing's base, then carried around in the normal way until it is directly below the hook shank. Only at this point is it pulled tight onto the wing. The direction of pull on the thread is straight down, so the twisting action that winding the thread produces is removed.

A winging loop is used to tie the wing firmly in an upright position.

1 Position the tying thread at the eye and collect the wing materials. Here, two matching slips of mallard primary are prepared. In this example the body and hackle have been omitted to help illustrate the method clearly.

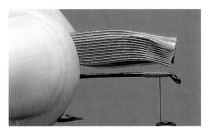

2 Make sure the slips are of equal width and place them together, dull sides in, so that the tips are level. Hold the slips over the top of the shank so that the butts are over the eye and the tips project just past the hook bend.

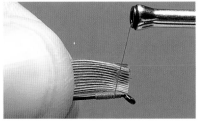

3 Drop the slips so that they sit on top of the hook. Raise the tying thread above the wing slips so that it forms a straight line in front of them.

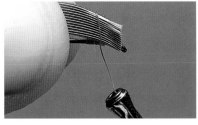

4 Keeping the tying thread loose, drop it behind the wing slips. Do not pull the thread tight at this point but position it directly beneath the hook shank and wing.

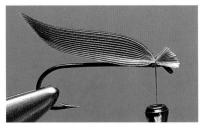

5 Still holding the wing slip in place, pull the thread tight in a straight, downward motion. This will compress the wing fibers directly onto the top of the hook. Remove the fingers and check the wing position.

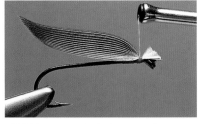

6 Add two more winging loops to make sure that the wing doesn't twist, then fix the wing in place with normal, tight thread wraps.

21

Collar hackles are used to suggest legs or wings, and to help the fly float and give it movement.

Collar hackles are usually tied with a soft-fibered cock hackle for nymphs (right) and wet flies (above).

► Forming a collar hackle

A collar hackle is used on many types of flies. Even where other styles of hackle are employed—such as a throat hackle—the base is often still a collar hackle. Therefore, it is important to have a basic grounding in this technique.

When tying any type of wound hackle, choosing the correct feather for the job is crucial. For dry flies, this usually means a stiff-fibered cock hackle, while for wet flies and other subsurface patterns a softer-fibered cock or hen hackle is required. For each of the flies featured in the book that include a collar hackle, the correct feather is specified.

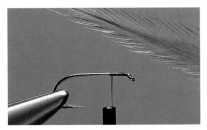

1 Choose the hackle, making sure that the fiber length is right for the hook. This will vary depending on the pattern, but for most dry flies it is around one-and-a-half to twice the width of the hook gape.

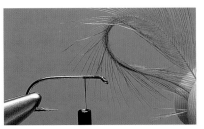

2 If you find it difficult to judge the fiber length, bending the hackle will cause the fibers to flare so that they can be seen more easily against the hook. Make sure that all the fibers over the main length are perfect.

3 Remove the fibers from a short length of the stem. Tear off any broken or otherwise damaged fibers.

4 With scissors, remove most of the bare stem to leave a short stub.

5 Using the bare stub of hackle stem, catch the hackle in position with two or three turns of tying thread. Take hold of the hackle tip with hackle pliers, clamping them firmly but gently onto the tip.

6 Wind on the hackle in closely butted turns toward the eye. Do not let the turns overlap as this will cause the fibers to twist out of position. To complete, secure the tip with thread and remove the excess hackle tip with scissors.

23

Tools

As with most crafts, fly-tying requires a range of tools designed to make the practitioner's life a little easier. They range from fundamentals, such as a vise and scissors, to optional tools, including the hair stacker and dubbing twister. While it is not imperative to obtain every tool listed here, they will help make the job of producing neat, well-tied flies more achievable.

Vise

While it is possible to hold the hook with your fingers, a purpose-designed vise will allow you to hold even small hooks firmly and securely. The vast majority of experienced fly-tyers wouldn't dream of not using one. Fly-tying vises are available in a range of designs, but they should all have a simple, sturdy action that will hold a variety of hooks firmly in the jaws so that they do not move. The preferred action of many tyers is a lever device that is pressed down once the vise jaws have been adjusted to suit the size of the hook. The jaws themselves should be hard-tempered in order to withstand many years of wear.

Dubbing Needle

This simple tool has a number of uses, including teasing out dubbing materials, dividing wing slips, and freeing trapped hackle fibers. It is also used to apply lacquer to the head of a fly.

Scissors

Another must-have tool. All that is required from a pair of fly-tying scissors is that they have sharp blades that are small enough to work closely around the hook. While it is possible to get away with a single pair, many experienced tyers have two. The first pair is the workhorse, used to cut through tough materials, such as feather stalks, hair, and tinsels. The second is kept sharp for the more delicate tasks, such as trimming hackle fibers, and usually has smaller, finer points than the first pair.

Hackle Pliers

Hackle pliers are available in a variety of forms, from simple sprung-metal types to those with a long, swiveled handle. The latter are easier to use, but the most important quality of any hackle pliers is that they have smooth, precise jaws that grip the hackle, or any other material, firmly without cutting. To this end, some models of hackle pliers have jaws covered with silicone rubber.

24

Bobbin Holder

It is possible to tie a fly by removing a length of tying thread from its spool; however, there are a number of advantages to be gained by using a specially designed bobbin holder. The foremost is that it allows the thread to be fed from the spool while it is wound around the hook, reducing waste to the bare minimum. Also, the weight of the bobbin holder, combined with the pressure that the arms exert on the spool, means that it can be released to hang beneath the hook while still retaining tension on the thread. The result is that the thread is prevented from unraveling without resorting to adding a half hitch after every tying procedure.

Dubbing Twister

When creating a dubbing loop, it is important to retain tension on the thread loop to keep the fur in position. Hackle pliers can be used, but the dubbing twister is far more efficient. With sprung-metal arms and a heavy circular body, it keeps the thread taut and can be easily spun, twisting the thread and dubbing into a rope.

Whip-finish Tool

A perfectly good whip finish can be executed with fingers alone; however, some tyers find this specially designed tool a great help. Models vary, but most whip-finish tools have a straight handle with a hook at one end and, lower down, a sprung-wire arm. The tying thread is positioned over the tool's hook and arm and the resulting loop wound around the fly hook.

Hair Stacker

When using hair to create wings, achieving the correct density can be a problem. Often the natural position of the hair on the skin means that the prepared wing will taper too much. However, the hair can be stacked so that the tips become level. The hair stacker is a metal or plastic tube into which the bunch of hair is placed, tips first. By tapping the stacker on a hard surface the hairs fall to the bottom, creating a level end to the wing.

Materials

Whereas the tools are the hardware of the fly-tying craft, the materials are what actually create the fly. You will find them in a mind-boggling range of colors and forms, from natural materials, such as hair, feather, and wool, to synthetics, including nylon, polypropylene, and Antron, to name but a few. As modern fly-tyers become more inventive, the list continues to grow. In fact, it is now so large and comprehensive that it would be impossible to list everything available without dedicating a whole book to the subject. For this reason, only a few of the most popular and widely used products are listed here. Even these are enough to tie hundreds of effective flies; and, from this starting point, you can build up your stock, over time, to encompass all the patterns that you intend to tie.

Tying Thread

Tying thread is used to secure the various components of a fly to the hook. It is available in a range of colors and diameters, with black 6/0 being the most commonly used. Finer threads, such as 8/0 and some of the superfine types, are used for small flies of size 16 and below. The heavier 3/0 diameter is used for large bucktails and streamers, where a strong thread is required to hold large bunches of hair and feather in place. Tying thread was originally made from silk, but today man-made materials, such as nylon and Kevlar, are used because they are strong, thin, and long lasting.

Tinsels

Tinsels are used to give a fly a degree of sparkle, either as a body or a rib. They are made from either metal or plastic. The metal type was once prone to tarnishing, but modern forms have a coat of varnish that helps them retain their sparkle for longer. Plastic tinsels, such as Mylar, never tarnish, but they are less robust than the metal types. Metal tinsels are available in gold, silver, and copper, while in plastic, pearl and holographic effects are now widely used.

Flosses

Like tying thread, floss was once only available in natural silk. Today, however, a variety of man-made products are also used. The color range is large, although black, red, yellow, and olive are the most popular. Single-ply

26

floss can be wound straight from the spool, while the two-ply floss must be divided into its component strands before being wound.

Yarns

Yarns, such as those made from polypropylene or Antron, can be found in a wide range of colors. Most can be used like floss, wound along the hook shank to create thick but smooth bodies. They are also used as wing posts for parachute flies or as tails on wet flies, streamers, and bucktails.

Beads

Small beads are commonly used in a wide range of nymph patterns and for a few streamers. Metal beads are available in a range of colors, including gold, silver, copper, and black, plus some fluorescent colors, such as orange and chartreuse. They are usually fixed at the hook eye, providing weight—particularly the tungsten beads—and, in the case of the more colorful types, a bit of sparkle. The lighter glass and plastic beads are used either to create the eyes on imitations of large nymphs or to add extra flash to the fly.

Dubbing Furs

Dubbing furs are used in a large number of patterns across the range of fly groups. Where once natural furs such as seal, hare, rabbit, and muskrat provided the main source, today man-made products such as polypropylene and Antron are widely used. Plain dyed colors are used alone or blended with other types of fur or iridescent strands to produce some wonderful effects.

Wing Quills

Wing quills such as those from the mallard duck or starling are used primarily as wet- or dry-fly wings, especially on patterns imitating small mayflies or midges. Normally used in the plain, natural gray form, they can also be found in white or a range of dyed colors.

Marabou

This soft, fluffy material once came from the marabou stork, but today its source is the white domestic turkey. Being white it is easily dyed, which makes it extremely versatile. That, and the fact that it is easy to use and has a superb action in the water, has made marabou the most popular winging material for a vast range of modern streamer patterns.

27

Hackles

The feathers from the neck and back of domestic poultry provide an important source of fly-tying materials. Known as hackles, they are used to suggest the legs of an insect or simply to add color and movement. The feathers from both cock and hen bird are used. Those from the hen are softer and more water absorbent, making them ideal for subsurface patterns, such as wet flies and nymphs. Prime-quality hackles from the cock bird have stiffer, less water-absorbent fibers, which is why they are most often used for tying dry flies. "Genetic" hackles, which have been purpose-bred to produce an extremely high-quality feather, are very long and thin, with the fibers close together. This makes them perfect for tying even very small dry flies. Lower-grade cock hackles are often used for hackles on streamers and bucktails or as streamer wings. Hackles come in a wide range of natural and dyed colors.

Hair

Various types of hair are used in fly-tying, the most popular application being as a wing on either hairwing or dry-fly patterns. The most widely used type of hair is that of the white-tailed deer. Known as bucktail, it is a strong, coarse hair, quite straight in the fiber, making it ideal for a whole range of medium to large patterns. Being white, it can also be readily dyed to provide a wide range of colors. Other types of hair used particularly for winging include squirrel tail and calf tail, both of which are finer than bucktail and better suited for use on smaller dry-fly patterns. Elk and deer body hair is also used for winging dry flies or, when spun and clipped, to form the buoyant Muddler head. When used still on the skin, rabbit and mink fur produce the classic Zonker style of tying used to create some highly effective baitfish imitations.

Peacock Herl

Peacock herl is a great material for making fly bodies, especially nymphs, dry flies, and wet flies. The iridescent fibers, though dark, give a beautiful sparkle while producing a chunky effect that imitates the profile of anything from a cased caddis larva to a beetle. Peacock herls are normally used as a body or thorax material, although strands are also included in the wing of some streamer patterns. The flue can also be removed and the quill used to form segmented fly bodies.

Feather Fiber

Various types of feather fiber are used for the bodies of both nymphs and dry flies. Though turkey, both plain and dyed, is popular, the most widely used feather fiber is taken from the tail of the male ring-necked pheasant. This chestnut feather is used for the classic Pheasant Tail Nymph, along with a range of other patterns, including the Teeny Nymph series. Now that pheasant tails can be bleached before being dyed, the versatility of the material has been increased and a whole range of natural and bright colors is now available.

Cul-de-canard

The soft, downy feather known as cul-de-canard (CDC) has been used in fly-tying for over 100 years, yet it is only in recent years that its popularity has spread around the world. Today, many tyers have come to realize how effective this material is, especially for tying dry flies. What makes cul-de-canard so special is that the feathers are located around the preen gland of a duck. As such, they are impregnated with oils that repel water but retain a soft, delicate texture. This makes them ideal for winging small mayfly and terrestrial imitations. In their natural form, CDC feathers are either gray, white, or pale brown, but they can be dyed and are now available in a wide range of colors.

Hooks

While materials such as hackles, dubbing, and yarn form the flesh and limbs of the fly, the hook provides the bones on which everything else hangs. Hooks are available in a wide variety of sizes and shapes, their use depending on the type of fly being tied. Most hooks have a single bend and point, but some trout and salmon hooks are manufactured as doubles or trebles with two or three points. For wet flies and nymphs, a heavy-wired model with a short shank is normally used to help the fly sink, while for dry flies lighter wire is used to keep weight to a minimum. For larger patterns, such as streamers, hairwings, some nymphs, and dry flies, longshanked hooks are used. This type of hook has a much longer shank, so while the gape of a size 8 longshank will be the same as that of a size 8 wet-fly hook, the shank may be twice the length.

Most trout hooks have a bronze finish, but those produced for tying salmon and steelhead flies are black. The eye of the hook is also different—instead of being created by bending the wire to the shank, they are formed as a tapered loop closed by winding on close turns of tying thread. Salmon hooks are also produced with an upturned eye.

29

CHAPTER ONE

DRY FLIES

Dry flies are designed to float on the water's surface. To achieve this, many are tied using materials that are either buoyant or that repel water. Man-made products, such as polypropylene, rayon, and Antron, are particular favorites because they are extremely light, while microcellular foam is increasingly used because it is so buoyant that it will keep any fly floating indefinitely.

In size and shape, dry flies vary greatly. They encompass any pattern that imitates an insect that either hatches on or falls onto the surface of a lake or river. Being aquatic, the adults of insect groups such as the mayflies, stoneflies, caddis flies, and midges, greatly influence the size and shape of many dry flies. However,

there is another group, the terrestrials, that is even more variable in form. In fly-fishing, the term terrestrial is used to describe any invertebrate that is not aquatic in either immature or adult forms. This can include anything from the smallest beetle or spider right up to chunky insects, such as grasshoppers and crickets.

Although many effective dry flies still have a traditional feel to them, modern materials and treatments have heavily influenced the group. With the advent of highly efficient modern spray and gel flotants, flies can be treated so that they float even without a hackle, relying simply on teased-out body materials or outstretched wings to keep them trapped in the surface film. The result is that slimmer, more lifelike patterns can be created—flies that will fool selective trout, even in clear, calm water.

F Fly

This is a simple but deadly little fly that works in a wide range of hatches. It can be tied in a variety of body colors to suggest anything from a small mayfly to a caddis fly, or even a stonefly. A small, black version is particularly effective when there are little dark-colored terrestrials on the water. The key to the pattern's success is a wing of natural gray cul-de-canard, which mimics the wing of the insect. Also its fibers, which are loaded with natural oil, keep the fly floating without the need for a hackle. The simplicity of this fly makes it easy to tie in even the smallest sizes, right down to a size 28 hook.

Brown
trout

Arctic
char

Cutthroat

Grayling

Rainbow
trout

Wing:
Natural gray
cul-de-canard

Thread:
Olive

Hook:
Size 10–28
fine wire

Body:
Olive pheasant
tail fibers

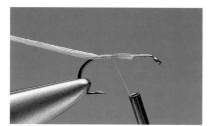 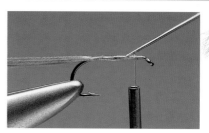

1 Fix the hook in the vise and run the tying thread along the shank from the eye to a point opposite the barb. Catch in four olive pheasant tail fibers with three firm turns of thread.

2 Allow the waste ends of the feather fibers to lie along the shank and cover them with thread to create an even base for the body. Apply a drop of clear lacquer.

 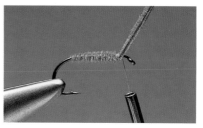

3 Leave the lacquer to dry until slightly tacky. Wind the feather fibers along the hook shank, keeping the turns even.

4 Continue winding the fibers to form an even body. Secure the loose ends with thread just behind the eye and trim off the excess with scissors.

5 Take two small cul-de-canard feathers and place them together so that their tips are level. Catch them in as a wing with three firm thread wraps behind the eye.

6 Position the wing low over the body, then trim off the excess feather with scissors. Secure with further tight thread wraps before casting off the thread with a whip finish.

33

Elk Hair Emerger

Brown trout

Rainbow trout

This simple, hackleless fly is tied specifically for fishing on lakes and reservoirs. It is designed to imitate a hatching chironomid midge, an insect that makes up a large part of the stillwater trout's diet. Because there isn't a hackle, the Elk Hair Emerger relies on its elk-hair wing and teased-out fur body to keep it floating. The body is applied by gently dubbing a small amount of fur onto the tying thread to form a thin, fluffy rope. Once applied, the point of a needle or a small piece of Velcro is used to rag the fur out slightly, making it more translucent and increasing its surface area. The Elk Hair Emerger is tied in a range of colors including fiery brown, orange, claret, and black.

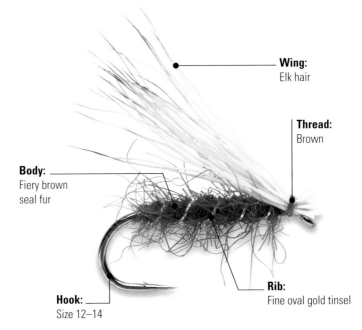

Wing:
Elk hair

Thread:
Brown

Body:
Fiery brown
seal fur

Rib:
Fine oval gold tinsel

Hook:
Size 12–14

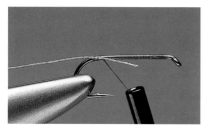

1 With the hook fixed in the vise, run the tying thread on at the eye and carry it down the shank to a point opposite the barb. Catch in 2 inches (5cm) of fine, oval, gold tinsel.

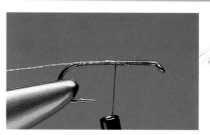

2 Using closely wound turns of tying thread, secure the waste end of the tinsel to the shank. This procedure ensures an even base to which the body can then be applied.

3 Take a pinch of fiery brown seal fur and apply it evenly to the thread. Dub it on with a simple finger-and-thumb twist and wind the resulting rope along the shank.

4 Stop the body a short distance from the eye, pinching away any excess fur. Take hold of the gold tinsel and wind five or six tight, evenly spaced turns over the body.

5 Secure and remove the loose tinsel end. Take a small bunch of elk hair, remove any broken fibers, and make sure that the tips are level. Catch it in place with tight thread turns so that the tips project just past the hook bend.

6 Secure with further turns of thread. Then, using slightly looser turns at the base, position the wing to sit at 45 degrees to the shank. Cast off the thread with a whip finish and trim the hair at the eye to leave a short stub.

35

Red Tag

Brown trout

Grayling

Rainbow trout

This is a very traditional little fly, most famous as a winter pattern for grayling. However, it is actually a very good general pattern, equally useful on rivers and lakes. Although most often used as a dry fly, it can also be tied to be fished wet, the only difference being that a softer-fiber hackle is used. An otherwise somber-hued fly, what really sets it off is the bright tag of red wool that gives the pattern its name. Tying a wool tail is not difficult; the main thing to watch out for is that the wool doesn't lead to an excessively bulky body. Because the body of the Red Tag is a chunky one of peacock herl, this isn't really an issue. Still, it pays to use the waste end of the wool, tied the length of the hook to form an even underbody.

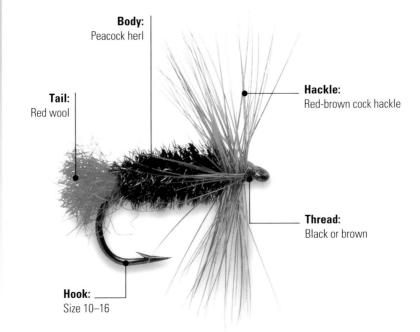

Body:
Peacock herl

Tail:
Red wool

Hackle:
Red-brown cock hackle

Thread:
Black or brown

Hook:
Size 10–16

1 With the hook fixed in the vise, run on the tying thread and carry it down the shank in touching turns. Take a short length of red wool and catch it in at a point opposite the barb.

2 Cover the waste end of the wool with close turns of thread, returning the thread to the bend. This will form an even base for the body. Tease out the wool fibers with the tip of a needle.

3 Trim the tail short, making a single, clean cut with a pair of scissors. Catch in three strands of peacock herl at the base of the tail.

4 Carry the tying thread up to the eye. Take hold of the peacock herls and twist them gently. Wind them along the shank to form a chunky body. For added strength, these herls can be wound over a layer of wet varnish.

5 Secure the herls in place a short distance from the eye and remove the excess.

6 Select a red-brown cock hackle with a fiber-length one-and-a-half times that of the hook gape. Catch it in at the eye and wind on three turns. Secure the end and trim the excess, then cast off.

Polywinged Midge

This little dry fly is effective and simple to tie. Tied in black it makes a great imitation of a whole host of small dark flies, from the black gnat and hawthorn fly to tiny black midges—all you do is alter the size of the hook. The Polywinged Midge consists of a body of dubbed fur, a wing of polypropylene, and a collar hackle to help it float. Dubbing is a basic process for applying a fur body, and entails twisting the teased-out fur along the thread between finger and thumb. Waxing the thread can help the fur adhere to it, and the fur is always twisted in the same direction to form a thin, fluffy rope.

Brown trout

Arctic char

Cutthroat

Grayling

Rainbow trout

Wing:
White siliconized polypropylene yarn

Body:
Black Antron

Hackle:
Black cock hackle

Thread:
Black

Hook:
Size 14–24

38

1 Having fixed the hook in the vise, wind the tying thread down the shank from the eye to the bend. Take a pinch of black Antron, tease it out, and apply loosely but evenly to the thread.

2 Between finger and thumb, gently twist the Antron onto the thread until a thin rope has been formed. Wind this rope along the hook shank, stopping just short of the eye.

3 Take a length of white polypropylene yarn and catch it in at the eye with three tight thread wraps.

4 Secure the yarn with further thread wraps and remove the excess with scissors. Select a black cock hackle with fiber length almost twice that of the hook gape.

5 Prepare the hackle by removing any soft or broken fibers from its base. Leave a short length of bare stem and catch this in, with thread, at the wing base.

6 Take hold of the hackle tip with a pair of hackle pliers. Wind on two turns of hackle and secure the tip with thread. Remove the excess hackle with scissors and cast off the thread.

39

Bi-Visible

Brown
trout

Rainbow
trout

Atlantic
salmon

Sea trout

The Bi-Visible is tied entirely from hackles—no other materials other than tying thread are used. The tail is a cock hackle point and the entire length of the hook is covered in close turns of hackle. Two different colors are always used, the darker at the rear followed by a distinct collar of white cock hackle just behind the eye. This combination produces the distinct bi-visible effect. Here it is tied in black and white, though a brown and white variation can also be tied. Being very bushy it is normally fished as a dry fly on fast, broken water where the dense hackles keep it riding high on the surface. It also makes a very good top-dropper fly when fishing a lake in a big wave.

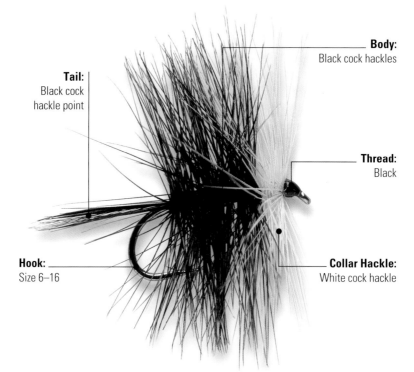

Body:
Black cock hackles

Tail:
Black cock
hackle point

Thread:
Black

Hook:
Size 6–16

Collar Hackle:
White cock hackle

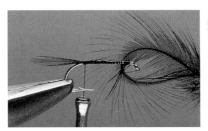

1 Fix the hook in the vise and run the tying thread on at the eye. Wind the thread in close turns, stopping at a point opposite the barb. Here, catch in a black cock hackle point as the tail.

2 Next, select another black cock hackle with fiber length approximately twice that of the hook gape. To judge this correctly, bend the hackle stem slightly. This will flare the hackle fibers and allow their length to be seen more easily.

3 Having selected the right size of hackle, remove any soft or broken fibers from its base and catch it in just in front of the tail. Grasp the hackle tip with a pair of hackle pliers and wind it up the shank in touching turns.

4 Once the hackle has been wound, fully secure the loose tip with turns of thread and remove the excess. Add further hackles in the same way, until three-quarters of the hook shank has been covered.

5 Select a pure white cock hackle with fibers slightly longer than those of the black hackles. Prepare this and catch it in just in front of the black hackles. Wind on close turns up to the eye.

6 Secure the hackle tip with turns of thread before removing the excess. Build a small, neat head and cast off the thread.

41

Griffith's Gnat

Brown
trout

Arctic
char

Cutthroat

Grayling

Rainbow
trout

Although called a gnat, this is actually a great all-purpose dry fly, effective either on rivers or lakes. It works best in smaller sizes where it suggests all sorts of small creatures trapped in the surface film. It also makes a very good representation of small chironomid midges in a mating ball. The Griffith's Gnat is tied using only two materials: peacock herl for the body and a grizzle cock hackle that is wound along its length. Interestingly, to keep weight to a minimum, there is no rib and the hackle is caught in at the tail and wound up toward the head, rather than the reverse. This hackle should also be very short, with fiber length little more than the gape of the hook.

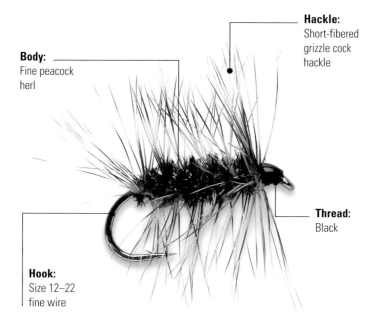

Hackle:
Short-fibered grizzle cock hackle

Body:
Fine peacock herl

Thread:
Black

Hook:
Size 12–22
fine wire

1 With the hook fixed in the vise, run the tying thread down the shank from the eye to opposite the barb. Select a marked grizzle cock hackle, preferably one from a genetic saddle patch.

2 Stroke the hackle fibers back against the grain to leave a short section of the tip. Trim this tip and catch the hackle in at a point opposite the barb.

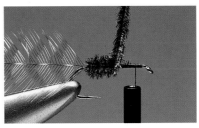

3 Select one or two peacock herls. Choose as slim a herl as possible to keep the finished body thin. Catch the herls in at the same point as the hackle. Wind the tying thread over the herl tips, stopping just short of the eye.

4 Take hold of the herls and, without twisting, wind them up to the eye. Secure the loose ends of the herls with thread and remove the excess with scissors.

5 Take hold of the hackle with a pair of hackle pliers and begin winding it toward the eye. Ensure that each turn of hackle is evenly spaced and that none of the fibers are trapped.

6 Carry the hackle right to the eye, then secure the waste end with thread and remove with scissors. Cast off the thread.

43

Brown
trout

Cutthroat

Grayling

Rainbow
trout

Elk Hair Caddis

Al Troth developed this superb imitation of an adult caddis fly. Rather than imitating a particular species, it uses the typical roof-wing profile to mimic a whole range of medium to small brown caddis flies. The wing is made from a small bunch of elk hock hair that has been bleached to a light tan. Elk hock is reasonably tough, but still retains some of the buoyancy found in ordinary elk hair. As when tying any hairwing, care must be taken to make the hair secure. Once the body and hackle are in place, the hair is presented to the hook so that the tips project just past the bend. Four tight turns of thread will lock the hair in place, with two or three slightly looser ones used to position the wing low over the body. After the thread is cast off, the excess hair can be trimmed off at the eye.

Wing:
Elk hock
hair

Body:
Dark hare's fur

Thread:
Brown

Rib:
Fine gold wire

Hook:
Size 12–14

Hackle:
Furnace cock
saddle hackle

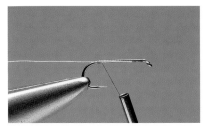

1 Once the hook is fixed in the vise, run the thread down the shank to a point opposite the barb, using tight, touching turns. Take 2 inches (5cm) of fine, gold wire and catch in place so the waste end lies the length of the shank.

2 Take a pinch of dark hare's fur and apply it to the tying thread. Dub it with finger and thumb to form a thin yarn. Wind the yarn to cover the full length of the hook.

3 Select a furnace cock saddle hackle. Prepare it by removing any broken fibers from the base to leave a short stub of bare stem.

4 Catch the hackle in at the eye by the section of bare stem. Gently hold the tip with a pair of hackle pliers and begin to wind the hackle in evenly spaced turns.

5 Once the hackle has reached the end of the body, take hold of the gold wire and wind it in evenly spaced turns up to the eye. This will hold the hackle turns in place.

6 Secure the wire with thread and remove the excess. Also remove the hackle tip with scissors. Secure a bunch of elk hock hair behind the eye as a wing. Trim the elk hair in front of the eye to leave a short stub, and cast off the thread.

Adams

Although now over eighty years old, the Adams is still a very modern looking fly. The combination of grizzle and brown hackles with a medium-gray body has produced a great general dry fly pattern that catches fish around the world in a wide range of water types. This makes the Adams one of the most popular trout flies in use today. This pattern uses hackle point wings along with two hackles wound together. Hackle point wings have the advantage that they are quick and easy to tie, and they don't rely on having to match up two slips of fragile feather.

Brown trout

Arctic char

Cutthroat

Grayling

Rainbow trout

Wing:
Grizzle hackle points

Body:
Gray muskrat
or rabbit

Thread:
Black

Hackle:
Brown and grizzle
cock hackles wound
together

Tail:
Brown and
grizzle hackle
fibers

Hook:
Size 10–20

1 With the hook fixed in the vise, run the tying thread a short distance down the shank. Select two grizzle hackle points and remove the base fibers so the tips are the same length as the hook.

2 Place the hackles together so that the tips are level. Catch the hackle in place by the bare sections of stem, a short distance from the eye.

3 Part the hackle points, using the tip of a needle if necessary. Pull the bare stems through the gap and secure with thread along the shank. This ensures the tips remain apart.

4 Remove any excess hackle stem, then run the tying thread down the shank. Take a few fibers of brown and grizzle hackle and catch them in place.

5 Offer a pinch of gray muskrat or rabbit underfur up to the thread. Dub it on to form a slim rope and wind up to the base of the wings to form the body.

6 Take two cock hackles, one brown, one grizzle, with fibers of equal length. Prepare them, leaving a short length of bare stem, and catch in behind the wing. Wind on four turns up to the eye. Secure with thread and remove the excess.

47

Light Cahill

Brown
trout

Cutthroat

Grayling

Rainbow
trout

The Light Cahill is a classic U.S. pattern and, though over 100 years old, is still a highly efficient fish catcher. It imitates a whole range of pale-colored mayflies, the most striking part of the fly being its speckled lemon wings. These wings are formed from fibers of lemon wood-duck flank feather, which are tied in as a single bunch and then divided to form a V-shaped profile. When tying this style of fly, the wing is normally applied before any other material. This allows the waste ends to be laid along the shank and then trimmed to a fine taper. The result is that bulk can be kept to a minimum and a slim body formed.

Wing:
Tufts of lemon
wood-duck flank

Hackle:
Light ginger or
cream cock hackle

Tail:
Cream hackle
feathers

Hook:
Size 12–18

Thread:
Yellow

Body:
Cream seal fur

1 Fix the hook in the vise and run the tying thread a short distance down the shank from the eye. Tear off a pinch of fibers from a lemon wood-duck feather. Making sure the tips are level, catch it in place.

2 For this style of wing, the fibers are tied in so that they project over the eye. Using figure-of-eight thread wraps, divide the wing into two equal bunches.

3 Extra turns of thread will bring the wings into an upright position. Trim off the butts to a taper and take the tying thread down to the bend. Catch in a few cream hackle fibers.

4 Having created a smooth, tapered underbody using tying thread, dub on a pinch of cream seal fur. Form a thin rope and wind it on to create a slim, tapered body. Stop the body at the point where the wing begins.

5 Prepare a cream cock hackle with fiber length one-and-a-half times the gape of the hook. Catch it in at the wing base.

6 Take hold of the hackle tip with hackle pliers and wind on three turns behind the wing. Make another two turns in front of the wing. Secure the hackle and remove the excess. Cast off.

49

Royal Wulff

First tied by the late Lee Wulff, the Royal Wulff is one of a series of dry flies that have a trademark V-shaped hair wing. The result is a fly that is robust and easy to tie. A bunch of bucktail or calf-tail hair is tied in so that it projects over the eye; it is then divided into two wings by using figure-of-eight turns of thread. With its striking coloration, the Royal Wulff is not an imitative pattern but rather it is used to trigger the trout's inquisitiveness. It is an effective fly even on hard-fished waters where trout become very selective. Other flies in the Wulff series include the Gray Wulff and the White Wulff, and the technique is now widely used to create a variety of medium to large mayfly imitations.

Brown trout

Arctic char

Cutthroat

Rainbow trout

Steelhead

Body:
Peacock herl and red floss

Wing:
White calf tail

Thread:
Black

Tail:
Brown bucktail

Hook:
Size 4–18

Hackle:
Brown cock hackle

1 Run the tying thread on at the eye, building a short section of close thread turns. Secure a bunch of white calf tail so that the tips project over the eye. Remove the waste ends, then divide the bunch with figure-of-eight thread wraps.

2 Wind the thread down the shank in touching turns, stopping at a point opposite the hook barb. Catch in a few fibers of brown bucktail as the tail allowing the waste ends to lie along the shank.

3 Secure the waste ends of the hair with open turns of thread. Then, at the base of the tail catch in two fibers of peacock herl. Wind them in close turns so that they cover one-third of the distance between the tail and the wing.

4 Secure the loose ends of the peacock herl and remove them. At the base of the first body section, catch in 2 inches (5cm) of red floss and wind it along the hook to form a section slightly longer than the one of peacock herl.

5 Add a second section of peacock herl between the red floss and the wing. Select a brown cock hackle with fibers approximately twice as long as the hook gape. Catch it in by its base to the rear of the wing.

6 Gripping the hackle tip with pliers, wind on three or four full turns to create a dense collar. Make a further two hackle turns in front of the wing, securing the tip and removing the excess. Build a neat head and cast off the thread.

Humpy

With its buoyant back and wing and dense hackle, the Humpy is a true high-float pattern designed for fishing fast, broken water. Although not tied as an imitation of any specific insect, it works as a good copy of many of the darker mayflies found on fast-flowing streams. Humpies are tied in a range of body colors. In each variation, the back and wing are tied from natural deer hair—the butts of the hair being used for the back while the tips are carried forward over the eye to form the wing. The trick is to judge the length of hair needed to create the back and leave enough length in the tips so the wing isn't too short.

Cutthroat

Rainbow trout

Atlantic salmon

Coho salmon

Steelhead

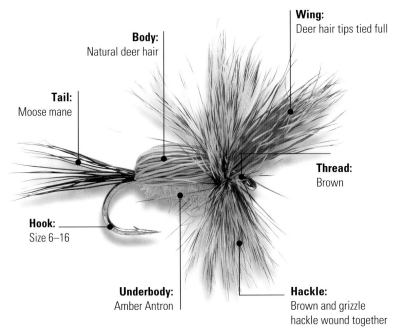

Wing:
Deer hair tips tied full

Body:
Natural deer hair

Tail:
Moose mane

Thread:
Brown

Hook:
Size 6–16

Underbody:
Amber Antron

Hackle:
Brown and grizzle hackle wound together

1 Fix the hook in the vise and run on the tying thread, stopping at a point opposite the barb. Take a few fibers of moose mane and, ensuring that the tips are level, catch them in at the bend. Trim away the waste ends.

2 Cut off a large bunch of deer hair and remove any broken fibers. Make sure that all the tips are level, and catch the bunch in so the waste ends lie along the shank.

3 Before fixing the hair properly in place, use the tying thread to pull it loosely over the eye to judge if the wing length is correct. It should be about the same length as the body. Release the deer hair.

4 Secure the deer hair, covering the waste ends with thread, then apply a pinch of amber Antron loosely to the thread at the tail. Dub it onto the thread to create a chunky rope, and wind it over the waste ends of the deer hair.

5 Pull the deer hair over the top of the body and secure in place a short distance from the eye. Remove any hairs that break or come loose.

6 Catch in either one long grizzle hackle or a grizzle and a brown hackle, and wind behind the wing to form a dense collar. Secure the tip with thread and remove, then cast off.

Highland Dun

Brown trout

Rainbow trout

This Australian pattern is designed to imitate the large, dark mayfly species found on that continent. It has a very traditional feel to it and uses slips of hen pheasant secondary feather for the wing plus a simple collar of dark brown cock hackle. The technique for tying this style of wing is employed in other traditional dry-fly patterns and involves taking slips from opposing wing feathers of birds such as the starling or mallard. In this instance, the slips are mottled hen pheasant placed together so the outer dull sides face one another. This allows the natural curves of the feathers to keep the slips apart in what is known as a split-wing style.

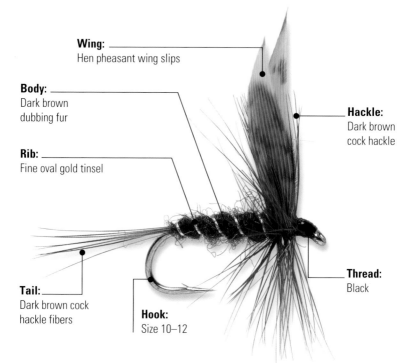

Wing:
Hen pheasant wing slips

Body:
Dark brown
dubbing fur

Hackle:
Dark brown
cock hackle

Rib:
Fine oval gold tinsel

Tail:
Dark brown cock
hackle fibers

Hook:
Size 10–12

Thread:
Black

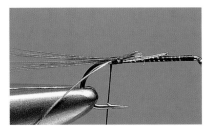

1 Fix the hook in the vise and run the tying thread down the shank from the eye to opposite the barb. Catch in a few fibers of dark brown cock hackle and 2 inches (5cm) of fine, oval, gold tinsel.

2 Wind close turns of thread over the waste ends of the hackle fibers and tinsel to provide an even base for the body. Dub on a pinch of dark brown fur and wind it on to form a slim body.

3 Wind on four turns of the gold tinsel and secure. Select two slips of hen pheasant feathers, taken from opposing wings. Place them together, dull-sides in, so that their tips are level and the feathers curve away from each other.

4 Catch in the hen pheasant wings with a winging loop just in front of the body.

5 Secure the wings with tight thread turns before trimming off the waste ends. Use turns of thread around the wing base to bring the wings upright.

6 Prepare a dark brown cock hackle with fibers twice the length of the hook gape. Catch it in at the wing base, and make three turns behind and two turns in front of the wing. Secure and remove the waste end before casting off.

55

Blue-winged Olive

Brown
trout

Cutthroat

Grayling

Rainbow
trout

Various species of mayfly throughout the world have the name Blue-winged Olive applied to them. They range in size from medium to small, but all have the same olive-colored body and thorax and smoky blue wings. This particular pattern is a thorax-tie version, so that rather than being wound in a tight collar, the hackle is spread in open turns over the length of the thorax. This gives a more natural footprint on the water, which is improved even further by clipping away the hackle fibers projecting beneath the hook. The body is constructed from a man-made fur such as Antron or polypropylene spun into a dubbing loop on fine 8/0 thread.

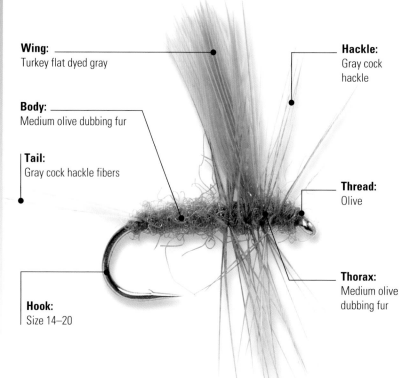

Wing:
Turkey flat dyed gray

Hackle:
Gray cock
hackle

Body:
Medium olive dubbing fur

Tail:
Gray cock hackle fibers

Thread:
Olive

Thorax:
Medium olive
dubbing fur

Hook:
Size 14–20

1 Run the tying thread from the eye to the bend. Dub on a small pinch of olive fur and wind on a few turns to form a tiny ball. Catch in a few fibers of gray cock hackle, winding the thread so that they push against the dubbing ball and splay out.

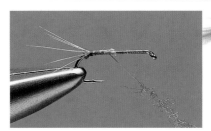

2 Wind the thread a short way back up the shank before applying another small pinch of medium olive fur to it. Make sure that the fur is evenly spread along the thread and that it tapers at the front.

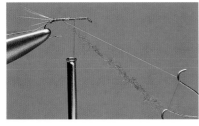

3 Place the two arms of a dubbing twister on the thread. Wind the loose end of the thread back onto the hook to form a loop.

4 Spin the dubbing twister to pull the two sides of the loop together, trapping the fur between, and creating a thin, tightly spun rope. Wind this rope two-thirds of the way along the hook to form the body.

5 Cut a slip of feather from a turkey flat that has been dyed gray. Fold the slip in half and catch it in as a wing just in front of the body. This wing should slope back over the body.

6 Catch in a gray cock hackle just in front of the body. Dub on a thorax of medium olive fur and use it to bring the wing to a more upright position. Wind on open turns of the hackle, securing and removing the tip at the eye. Cast off.

CDC Dun

Brown
trout

Cutthroat

Grayling

Rainbow
trout

Tied in a variety of sizes and shades of olive, the CDC Dun is
a wonderfully effective imitation of a whole range of small to
medium mayfly species. The gray cul-de-canard wing provides
just the right color and translucency to suggest those of the
freshly emerged mayfly dun, producing a pattern that can be tied
on with confidence when fishing either rivers or lakes. The key
when tying small dry flies is to keep the effect as slim and sparse
as possible. Here, this is achieved by using a split-thread dubbing
technique for the body rather than a dubbing loop. It allows a
tightly spun body to be formed while keeping bulk to a minimum.

Wing:
Natural gray cul-de-canard

Hackle:
Blue-gray
cock hackle

Body and Thorax:
Olive dubbing fur

Tail:
Blue-gray cock
hackle fibers

Thread:
Olive

Hook:
Size 12–20 fine wire

58

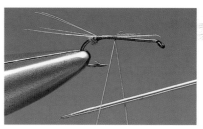

1 Run the tying thread along the shank to the bend. Dub on a pinch of olive fur and wind on a few turns to form a tiny ball. Catch in a tail of four blue-gray cock hackle fibers, winding the thread so that they push against the ball of fur and splay out.

2 Take the thread over the waste ends of the hackle fibers, then split the thread with the tip of a needle. Dividing the thread in this manner allows a very fine dubbed body to be formed.

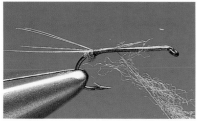

3 Keeping the two parts of the strand apart, position a small pinch of olive fur between them. Aim to apply the fur thinly and evenly.

4 Spin the bobbin holder. The effect is similar to using a dubbing twister, spinning the thread and fur together to create a tight yarn. Wind the spun fur along the shank to form a slim body.

5 With the body covering two-thirds of the hook shank, take a pinch of natural gray cul-de-canard and catch it in so that it slopes back slightly over the body.

6 Catch in a blue-gray cock hackle a short distance behind the wing. Dub on a thorax of olive fur and wind the hackle in open turns over it. Secure the hackle tip at the eye and remove it, then cast off.

59

Parachute Hare's Ear

When trout are repeatedly rising with a gentle sipping action, this is certainly the pattern to try. Tied parachute style, this version of the ever-popular Hare's Ear is absolutely deadly when fish are feeding on insects trapped in the surface. The thing that sets parachute flies apart is the way the hackle is tied. Instead of being wound around the hook, the hackle is applied around a wing post, which sits upright at 90 degrees to the hook shank. This post can be constructed from a variety of materials, such as foam or polypropylene yarn. Here a bunch of calf hair is used with close turns of tying thread wound around its base to increase rigidity and provide a solid base for the hackle.

Brown trout

Cutthroat

Grayling

Rainbow trout

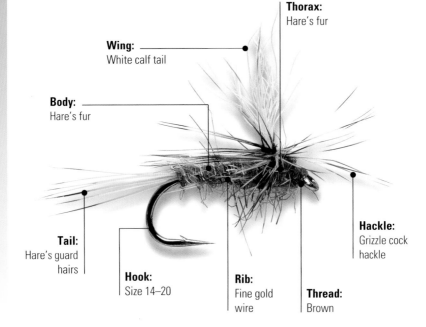

Thorax:
Hare's fur

Wing:
White calf tail

Body:
Hare's fur

Tail:
Hare's guard hairs

Hook:
Size 14–20

Rib:
Fine gold wire

Thread:
Brown

Hackle:
Grizzle cock hackle

1 Fix the hook in the vise. Run the tying thread on at the eye and carry it a short distance down the shank. Remove a small bunch of calf tail, make sure the tips are level, and catch it in place.

2 In this style of wing, the hair is first tied in tips over the eye. Secure it in place with tight thread wraps, lifting the hair upright by winding thread around its base.

3 Trim the waste end of the hair and carry the thread down to a point opposite the barb. Catch in a few fibers of hare's guard hair and 2 inches (5cm) of fine, gold wire.

4 Dub on a body of hare's fur up to the wing and rib it with wraps of wire. Select a grizzle cock hackle with fibers as long as the body. Remove any broken fibers from the base to leave a stub of bare stem. Catch the hackle in at the wing base.

5 Grasp the tip of the hackle with a pair of hackle pliers. Wind three turns around the base of the wing post. Catch in the hackle tip with thread and remove the excess.

6 Stroke the hackle fibers back away from the eye and dub on a small pinch of hare's fur. Wind this on in front of the wing, carrying it right to the eye. Cast off the thread.

61

Klinkhammer Special

Hans van Klinken devised this novel-looking fly that takes the parachute hackle technique to another level. The profile is intended to represent that of an emerging caddis fly with the body of the pupa sitting under the surface while the hackle and wing make sure that the fly floats. The fly is tied on a curved, caddis hook that has its shank bent with pliers to give a flat base for the thorax and wing. Body color may be varied from tan and olive to black, and the wing can be tied from materials such as cul-de-canard or polypropylene.

Brown trout

Grayling

Rainbow trout

Wing:
Gray cul-de-canard

Hackle:
Blue-gray cock hackle

Body:
Tan dubbing fur

Thread:
Black

Thorax:
Peacock herl

Hook:
Size 12–22 curved caddis hook bent slightly halfway along the shank

1 Fix the hook in the vise and use fine-nose pliers to bend down the front section of the shank by a few degrees.

2 Run on the thread just short of the eye, and carry it down the shank and around the hook bend. Dub a pinch of tan fur onto the thread. Wind the dubbed thread around the shank to form a slim body, stopping at the new bend made in step 1.

3 Take the thread back toward the eye and catch in four gray cul-de-canard plumes that have been placed together so that their tips are level. Wind the thread around the base of the feathers to bring them upright.

4 Catch in two strands of peacock herl in front of the body and gently twist them together to form a rope. Wind the rope up to the wing base. Do not remove the ends at this point.

5 Prepare a blue-gray cock hackle, leaving a short length of bare stem, and catch it in at the base of the wing. Using hackle pliers, make three or four turns of the hackle just above the turns of peacock herl.

6 Secure the hackle point with thread and remove the excess. Stroke the fibers back and wind the remaining peacock rope to the eye. Secure the loose end and remove the excess before stroking the hackle into position. Cast off.

63

Daddy Longlegs

Brown trout

Rainbow trout

Sea trout

The crane fly, or daddy longlegs, is a semiaquatic insect that can be found throughout the summer and fall, though it is during the cooler months toward the end of the year that it is most prolific. The larvae live either in bankside soil or in the damp margins of either rivers or lakes, where they feed on the roots of vegetation. Though the adults vary in size and color, they all have the characteristically thin, tapered body and long, gangling legs. These legs are a major recognition point for the trout, and for any imitation to be successful they must be included. Various materials have been used to imitate these legs, ranging from horsehair to nylon monofilament. Here, cock pheasant tail fibers have been used, each knotted twice to suggest the joints.

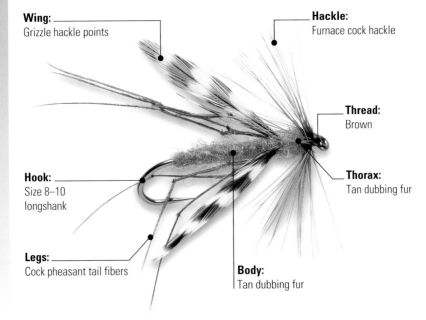

Wing:
Grizzle hackle points

Hackle:
Furnace cock hackle

Thread:
Brown

Hook:
Size 8–10
longshank

Thorax:
Tan dubbing fur

Legs:
Cock pheasant tail fibers

Body:
Tan dubbing fur

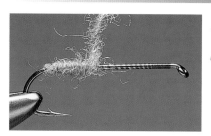

1 Fix the hook in the vise and run the tying thread from the eye to opposite the barb. Offer up a pinch of tan dubbing fur to the thread.

2 Dub the fur onto the thread with a simple finger-and-thumb twist. Create a thin rope and wind it in touching turns to cover two-thirds of the shank.

3 Take a single strand of cock pheasant tail and make a simple overhand knot in it. Draw this knot tight to create a kink that mimics the joint in the insect's leg.

4 Add a second knot a short distance back from the first to suggest two joints. Repeat this process to create six legs.

5 Split the six legs into two groups of three. Catch the groups in on both sides of the body so that they trail back past the hook bend. Trim the waste ends.

6 Add wings of grizzle hackle points plus a thorax of the same tan dubbing fur used for the body. Finish off with a collar of furnace cock hackle and cast off.

Gum Beetle

Brown trout

Rainbow trout

Microcellular foam is a wonderful material for creating beetle imitations. The buoyancy of the foam means that the beetle will float right in the surface film without the need for a hackle or an added floatant. The foam is available in sheets of various thicknesses, the most useful for this size of fly being ⅛ inch (3mm). Colors also vary, yellow being the base for this Gum Beetle, which is a favorite Australian pattern. Black, however, is the most commonly used color because it imitates any of the small black beetles found throughout the world. The width of the strip used depends on the size of the hook—for a size 10, ⅜ inch (10mm) will provide the correct profile and buoyancy.

Back:
Closed-cell foam, colored an iridescent green

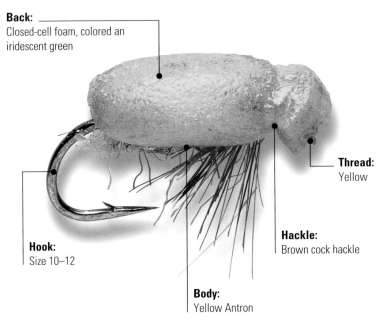

Thread:
Yellow

Hackle:
Brown cock hackle

Hook:
Size 10–12

Body:
Yellow Antron

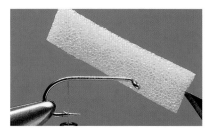

1 Fix the hook in the vise and run the tying thread from the eye to the bend. Using a sharp blade, cut a section of yellow foam 1 inch (2.5cm) long and ⅜ inch (10mm) wide.

2 Catch in the foam so the waste end covers three-quarters of the shank and fix with turns of thread. Don't wind the thread turns too close over the foam because this will compress it and reduce buoyancy.

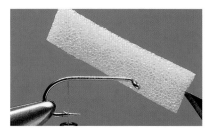

3 With the thread back at the bend, dub on a body of yellow Antron to cover the waste foam.

4 Wind on a few turns of brown cock hackle to suggest the beetle's legs, then pull the foam over the body and secure it with thread slightly back from the eye. Remember not to stretch the foam too much because this also reduces buoyancy.

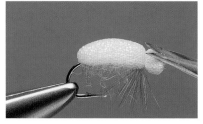

5 Cast off the tying thread with a whip finish and trim the head to a round shape.

6 Color the foam with green and orange marker pens to copy the colors of the real beetle. Finally, give the back a coat of clear varnish to protect it.

Stimulator

Cutthroat

Rainbow
trout

Coho
salmon

Steelhead

The Stimulator is a large, high-float fly with a low-wing profile that mimics a variety of caddis and stonefly species. With a tail and wing of buoyant elk hair, it can be fished dead-drift or skated without swamping, even in fast, broken water. Positioning can be a problem when tying in elk because it is hollow and easily compressed, so tight turns of thread will cause it to flare. Tight turns are therefore only used to fix the hair in place. Once this has been achieved, looser turns are used around the wing base to position it low over the body. Laying the first turn of the dubbed thorax over the wing will also help achieve this profile.

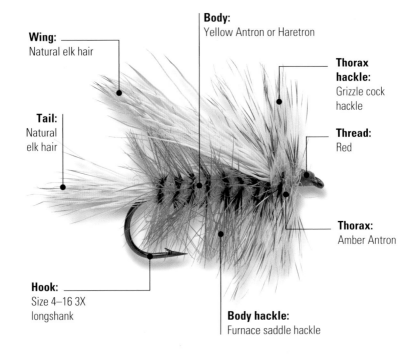

Wing:
Natural elk hair

Body:
Yellow Antron or Haretron

Thorax hackle:
Grizzle cock hackle

Tail:
Natural elk hair

Thread:
Red

Thorax:
Amber Antron

Hook:
Size 4–16 3X longshank

Body hackle:
Furnace saddle hackle

1 Fix the hook in the vise and wind red tying thread down the hook shank in touching turns. At the bend, catch in a bunch of natural elk hair that has been prepared by removing any base fluff and broken fibers.

2 Secure the hair in place with four tight turns. Use the waste ends to form an even base for the body, covering them with thread. Return the thread to the bend. Take a furnace saddle hackle, stroke the fibers back, and catch in by its tip.

3 Dub on a body of yellow Antron and wind three-quarters of the way along the hook. Take hold of the hackle with a pair of hackle pliers and wind it over the body in evenly spaced turns. Secure the waste end and remove the excess.

4 Take a second, larger bunch of elk hair. Prepare it in the same way as before and fix in position to the front of the body. Use tight thread wraps to lock in place, then two or three looser turns to position it.

5 Remove any excess hair with scissors; then, at the front of the wing, catch in a grizzle cock hackle. Dub on a pinch of amber Antron and wind on the resulting yarn to form the thorax.

6 Finally, take hold of the hackle tip with hackle pliers and wind on three full turns. Secure the tip with thread wraps and remove the excess. Build a small head and cast off the thread with a whip finish.

69

Dave's Hopper

Brown trout

Cutthroat

Rainbow trout

This brilliant imitation of a grasshopper was developed by top American fly-tyer Dave Whitlock, who is responsible for a number of other extremely effective patterns. It is a complicated pattern to tie, but well worth the effort, as it is deadly during high summer when trout are feeding on the natural hoppers. The wing is fashioned from a folded strip of turkey wing quill. To make sure that it retains its shape over many casts and fish, spray the back of the quill with a fixative such as Feather Weld to strengthen it. The hopper's two long jumping legs are imitated by tying knots in strips of golden pheasant tail feather. These knots put a bend in the feather and give the impression of a leg joint. The head is constructed Muddler-style from spun and clipped deer hair, but cut to the blunt head shape of the grasshopper.

Legs:
Golden pheasant
tail feather

Wing:
Lacquered turkey
wing quill

Head:
Natural gray
deer hair

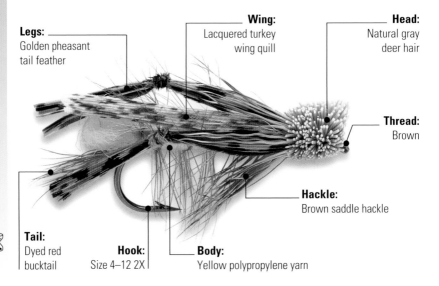

Thread:
Brown

Hackle:
Brown saddle hackle

Tail:
Dyed red
bucktail

Hook:
Size 4–12 2X

Body:
Yellow polypropylene yarn

1 Secure the hook in the vise and run the tying thread from the eye to the bend. Catch in a tuft of dyed red bucktail and a loop of yellow polypropylene yarn. Allow the waste ends of both to lie along the shank.

2 At the base of the tail, catch in a brown saddle hackle by its tip along with 4 inches (10cm) of yellow yarn. Cover the waste ends of the previous materials with thread, then wind on the yarn in close turns to form the body.

3 Stop the yarn three-quarters of the way along the shank. Secure the loose end and remove with scissors. Wind the hackle in evenly spaced turns down the entire length of the body.

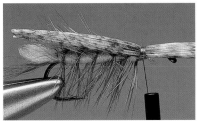

4 Secure the loose hackle end and remove. Spray the back of a mottled turkey wing quill with a flexible fixative and allow to dry. Remove a slip three times the width of the intended wing. Roll the slip and fix in place on top of the body.

5 Take two bunches of golden pheasant tail feather. Make a simple overhand knot in each and trim the tips so they are the same length. Catch them in on both sides of the body to mimic the hopper's jumping legs.

6 Trim off the waste ends of the legs before adding a head of natural gray deer hair spun and trimmed in the standard Muddler technique. Cast off and trim the front end of the head square to give the same profile as the real hopper.

71

Balloon Caddis

Austrian angler Roman Moser devised this wonderful imitation of a caddis fly pupa at the very point of transposing into the adult. Rather than use a hackle to keep the fly floating, Roman went for a more modern approach with closed-cell foam. The foam provides the required buoyancy, but also mimics perfectly the bulge in the thorax as the adult caddis fly pulls itself from the pupal shuck. When using foam, the key is never to pull it too tight. Stretching will reduce the material's natural buoyancy and might well mean that it won't keep the fly afloat. The Balloon Caddis can be tied in a range of body colors, including amber and pale green. Effective hook sizes range from an 8 to a 16.

Brown trout

Cutthroat

Grayling

Rainbow trout

Wing:
Brown elk hair

Thorax:
Yellow closed-cell foam

Hook:
Size 8–16

Body:
Olive Antron or Irisé Dub

Thread:
Yellow

1 Fix the hook in the vise and run the tying thread in touching turns to a position opposite the barb. Offer up a large pinch of olive Irisé Dub to the thread. Apply it so that it forms a loose yarn.

2 Make one turn of the yarn at the bend to lock the fibers. Continue twisting to form a strong, thick yarn, then cover two-thirds of the shank with it.

3 With the body in place add tight thread turns to form a base for the wing. Remove a pinch of brown elk hair, making sure that the tips are reasonably level.

4 Hold the hair on top of the hook and fix in place with three or four tight thread wraps. This will make the hair flare out. Secure with further tight turns and trim off the waste hair at the front.

5 Position the hair low over the hook with loose turns made at the wing base. Next, cut a thin strip of yellow foam and catch it in place at the eye. Wind the thread over the waste end of the foam, bringing it to the base of the wing.

6 Pull the foam back over the wing to form a pronounced thorax and secure with thread. Trim off the excess and cast off.

73

Sparkle Dun

Brown trout

Arctic char

Cutthroat

Grayling

Rainbow trout

No-hackle flies are designed for fishing smooth glides and other types of water where trout are suspicious of denser, hackled patterns. The Sparkle Dun is a variation on the original Compara Dun, with a tail of clear Antron replacing the natural, gray deer hair. The aim is to imitate a small mayfly emerging from its nymphal shuck, and the clear, sparkling tail does this superbly. The fly is made to float by using deer hair flared around the top of the hook in a semicircle. The hollow deer hair provides both buoyancy and the profile of an up-winged mayfly. The Sparkle Dun can be tied in a wide range of sizes to imitate the various mayfly species.

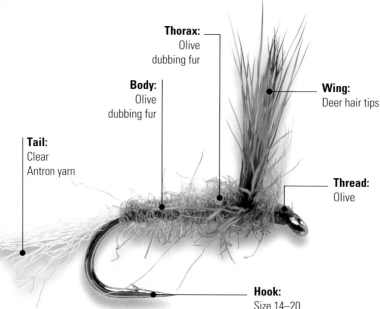

Thorax:
Olive
dubbing fur

Body:
Olive
dubbing fur

Wing:
Deer hair tips

Tail:
Clear
Antron yarn

Thread:
Olive

Hook:
Size 14–20

1 Fix the hook in the vise. Run the tying thread on at the eye and wind on close turns to a third of the way down the shank, to form a solid base for the wing. Take a pinch of deer hair and hold it so that the tips are level.

2 Offer the hair up to the hook so the tips project over the eye, bearing in mind that the wing should be slightly shorter than the hook's length. Wind on two loose thread turns.

3 Secure the wing in place with further tight thread wraps. Use scissors to trim away the hair butts to form a slight taper.

4 Cover the butts of the deer hair with close turns of thread, carrying it down to the bend. At this point, catch in a few fibers of clear Antron as the tail.

5 Take a pinch of olive dubbing fur and apply it loosely to the thread. Dub it, twisting the fur onto the thread between finger and thumb, to form a thin yarn. Wind the yarn up to the wing.

6 Dub a second, smaller pinch of fur onto the thread. Push the deer hair back, so that it forms a semicircle, and wind the fur in front to fix in place.

Goddard Caddis

This pattern was originally known as the G&H Sedge, after its inventors, John Goddard and Cliff Henry. It uses deer hair clipped into the roof-winged profile of an adult caddis fly. The result is not only a very natural shape, but also the buoyancy of the deer hair means that the fly floats like a cork, even when being skated over the surface. The deer hair is applied in exactly the same way as it would be for a Muddler Head, the only difference being that it runs the entire length of the hook shank. When applying deer hair always use a good strong tying thread. This allows plenty of pressure to be applied, so that the hair will flare properly around the hook.

Brown trout

Cutthroat

Rainbow trout

Atlantic salmon

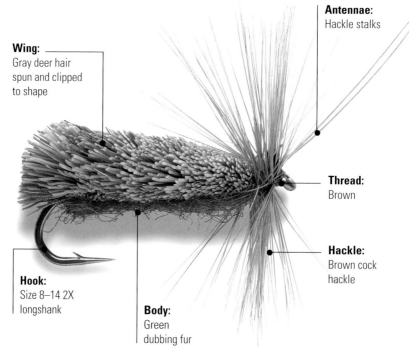

Antennae:
Hackle stalks

Wing:
Gray deer hair spun and clipped to shape

Thread:
Brown

Hackle:
Brown cock hackle

Hook:
Size 8–14 2X longshank

Body:
Green dubbing fur

76

1 With the hook fixed in the vise, run the tying thread down the shank from the eye to the bend. Take a pinch of gray deer hair. Hold it parallel to the hook shank and wind two loose thread turns over it.

2 Pull the thread tight. As this happens, the soft deer hair will flare around the hook shank. If necessary, ease it around with the fingers.

3 Once the deer hair has formed an even ruff around the hook, fix it in position with tight thread turns, both through and in front of the hair. Continue adding further small bunches of deer hair until the hook shank is covered, then cast off.

4 With a pair of scissors begin to trim the hair into a caddis fly profile, cutting the hair much shorter beneath the hook shank than above it.

5 When a satisfactory profile has been achieved, run the tying thread back on at the bend and fix a body of dubbed green fur under the wing.

6 Next, add two hackle stalks as the antennae, and a brown cock collar hackle. Cast off the tying thread.

Turck's Tarantula

Devised by Guy Turck, this unorthodox fly has the distinction of winning the prestigious Jackson Hole One Fly competition. It combines a number of elements, such as its low calf-tail wing and Muddler head, along with rubber legs, to produce a large, dry fly that rises big, selective trout, even on hard-fished waters. Because it has plenty of built-in action, it can be fished in a whole manner of ways, from dead drift to twitched or skated. It is tied in a range of body colors from hare's fur to red, green, and tan. Being buoyant, it can also be fished with a small, weighted nymph tied to a dropper off the bend.

Brown trout

Cutthroat

Rainbow trout

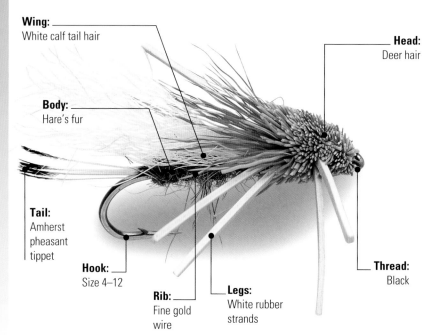

Wing: White calf tail hair

Head: Deer hair

Body: Hare's fur

Tail: Amherst pheasant tippet

Hook: Size 4–12

Rib: Fine gold wire

Legs: White rubber strands

Thread: Black

1 Once the hook is fixed in the vise, run the tying thread from just short of the eye to opposite the barb. Catch in a few strands of Amherst pheasant tippet and 2 inches (5cm) of fine, gold wire.

2 Take a good pinch of hare's fur and rub it in the palm of the hand to mix the fiber directions. Dub the fur thickly onto the thread and wind it two-thirds of the way along the shank. Wind the gold wire over the body in evenly spaced turns.

3 Tease out any fluff or broken fibers from a bunch of white calf tail hair and catch it in as a wing. This wing should lie low over the body, with its tips level with those of the tail.

4 Cut a bunch of deer hair from the skin. Catch it in so that the tips lie back over the wing. Using tight thread turns, spin the hair around the shank so that the tips form a ruff.

5 Take four white rubber strands and catch two in on both sides of the deer-hair head. This produces a wonderful action on the water that makes the fly so effective.

6 Spin a second bunch of deer hair between the strands, plus another between the front strands and the eye. Cast off the thread with a whip finish before carefully trimming the hair to form a Muddler head.

79

Polywinged Spinner

Brown trout

Cutthroat

Rainbow trout

Instead of having a hackle, the Polywinged Spinner relies on outstretched wings to keep it afloat. The profile mimics that adopted by a female mayfly lying spent, having laid her eggs. Polypropylene yarn is used because it is very light and repels water, especially if pretreated with a siliconized floatant. To keep the tail end of the fly from sinking, a few fibers of cock hackle are used. These are kept in a splayed position by adding a tiny ball of dubbing. Hackleless patterns of this type are normally tied on small, lightweight hooks ranging from a size 14 down to a 24 or smaller, depending on the species being imitated.

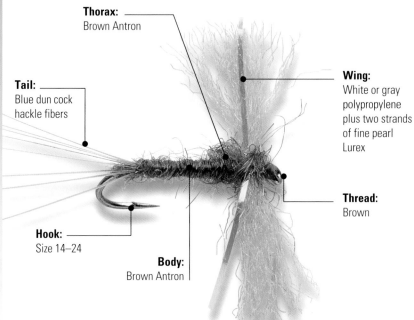

Thorax:
Brown Antron

Tail:
Blue dun cock hackle fibers

Wing:
White or gray polypropylene plus two strands of fine pearl Lurex

Thread:
Brown

Hook:
Size 14–24

Body:
Brown Antron

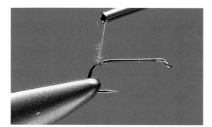

1 With the hook fixed in the vise, run the tying thread in touching turns down the shank to a point opposite the barb. Dub on a tiny amount of brown Antron and wind on a small ball.

2 Catch in four fibers of blue dun cock hackle as a tail. Wind the thread so the fibers are forced down on the dubbing ball. This will cause them to splay out.

3 Dub on a larger pinch of brown Antron. Wind it over the shank, stopping short of the eye, to form a very slim body.

4 Take a length of white or gray polypropylene yarn and secure it in front of the body with figure-of-eight thread wraps so that it lies at right angles to the hook shank.

5 Take a strand of fine, pearl Lurex and catch it in so that it lies along the length of the polypropylene yarn wings. Secure with further turns of thread.

6 Trim the wings so that each is the same length as the body. Finally, dub on a third pinch of Antron and wind around the wing base. Cast off.

81

Shipman's Buzzer

Brown
trout

Rainbow
trout

Dave Shipman originated this "damp," dry fly designed to sit right in the surface film. The pattern is tied to imitate a hatching midge, and the white Antron breathers at either end of the body keep it floating. In order to increase surface area, the body can be roughed up a little with a piece of Velcro before a flotant is applied. Although really a stillwater pattern, when tied on small hooks, from a size 18 down, it works well in running water, particularly on calm glides and glassy pools. The Shipman's Buzzer is tied in a range of colors, with black, olive, and orange being the most popular. A thin rib of pearl Lurex is usually incorporated to suggest the sparkling gases trapped under the skin of the hatching midge pupa.

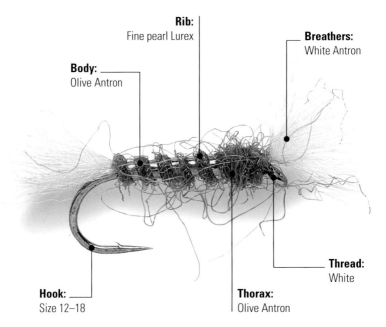

Rib:
Fine pearl Lurex

Breathers:
White Antron

Body:
Olive Antron

Hook:
Size 12–18

Thorax:
Olive Antron

Thread:
White

82

1 With the hook fixed in the vise, run the tying thread from the eye to opposite the barb. Wind it back to the eye and catch in a length of white Antron so that the ends project over both ends of the hook.

2 Carry the thread down to the bend, making close turns over the Antron. Pulling the Antron tight at this point will help reduce bulk.

3 Catch in 2 inches (5cm) of fine pearl Lurex. Dub a pinch of olive Antron evenly onto the tying thread and wind it along the hook toward the eye.

4 Stop winding the dubbing a short distance back from the front tuft of white Antron. Take hold of the Lurex and wind it in open, evenly spaced turns over the body.

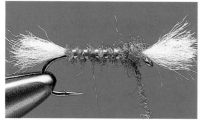

5 Secure the loose end of Lurex with tying thread and remove. Take a second, smaller pinch of olive Antron, dub it onto the thread, and wind it on to form the thorax.

6 Cast off with the usual whip finish. Trim the breathers at either end, if necessary, before roughing up the body with Velcro.

83

Shuttlecock

Brown
trout

Rainbow
trout

This is a classic Emerger pattern in the same style as the
Klinkhammer Special. However, the Shuttlecock is tied without a
hackle, relying on its wing of gray cul-de-canard feather to keep
it floating. The wing projects so far forward that the body
actually sinks beneath the surface and mimics that of a
chironomid midge pupa on the very point of transposing into the
adult. Because it is imitating a relatively small insect, the
Shuttlecock is most effective tied on hooks from size 14 down to
an 18, and for river use this can be as low as a 24. Body color
varies from black, olive, and fiery brown to red and orange.

Wing:
Natural gray
cul-de-canard feather

Thorax:
Orange Antron

Body:
Black rabbit fur

Rib:
Fine pearl
Lurex

Hook:
Size 14–24

Thread:
Orange

84

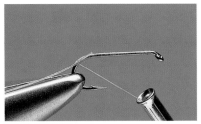

1 Fix the hook in the vise and run the tying thread on at the eye. Wind it down the shank in touching turns, carrying it slightly around the bend. Catch in 2 inches (5cm) of fine, pearl Lurex.

2 Take a small pinch of black rabbit fur and dub it thinly onto the thread with a simple finger-and-thumb twist. Wind the fur along three-quarters of the hook shank to form a slim body.

3 Wind the pearl Lurex along the body in close, evenly spaced turns.

4 Secure the Lurex with thread and remove the waste end. Select a natural gray cul-de-canard feather. Ideally, the feather should have plenty of soft fibers.

5 Select another two cul-de-canard feathers of a similar size and color, and place all three together so that their tips are level. Catch them in at the eye so that the tips project forward, over the eye.

6 Secure the feathers with tight thread wraps before removing the waste ends with scissors. Wind on a thorax of dubbed orange Antron and cast off with a whip finish.

85

Brown trout

Arctic char

Cutthroat

Grayling

Rainbow trout

DRY FLIES

CDC Emerger

Cul-de-canard is a wonderful material for tying both dry flies and emergers. The feather comes from around the preen gland of a duck, and its fibers contain many tiny filaments impregnated with the natural oil of the duck. This means that cul-de-canard floats superbly, as do the flies tied with it. The CDC Emerger imitates a small mayfly nymph at the very point of transition into the winged adult. Its looped back sits right in the surface film producing a lifelike imitation of this most vulnerable stage in the insect's life.

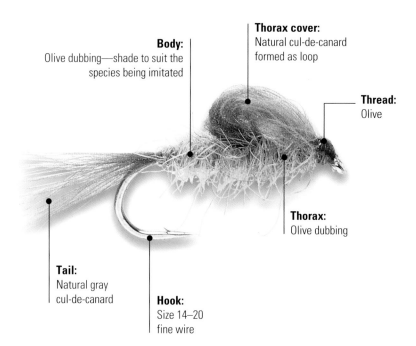

Body:
Olive dubbing—shade to suit the species being imitated

Thorax cover:
Natural cul-de-canard formed as loop

Thread:
Olive

Thorax:
Olive dubbing

Tail:
Natural gray cul-de-canard

Hook:
Size 14–20 fine wire

1 Fix the hook in the vise. Run the tying thread on at the eye and wind it down the shank in close turns to a point opposite the barb. Take a pinch of gray cul-de-canard fibers and catch it in as the tail.

2 Tease out a pinch of olive Antron dubbing fur and apply it thinly to the tying thread. Twist it into a slim rope and wind it two-thirds of the way to the eye.

3 Choose two cul-de-canard plumes of equal size and of the same shade of gray. Put them together so that their tips are level and secure just in front of the body with a few turns of thread.

4 Take a second pinch of olive Antron and apply it to the tying thread. Wind the fur up to the eye to form a distinct thorax.

5 With the tying thread just behind the eye, take a needle and loop the cul-de-canard plumes around it. Keeping tension on the loop, secure the butts with thread at the eye.

6 With the looped back formed, remove the excess plumes with scissors. Finally, build a small, neat head with the thread before casting off with a whip finish.

87

Detached Body Mayfly

Brown trout

Cutthroat

Rainbow trout

When tying imitations of large insects, such as the daddy longlegs and some of the bigger species of mayfly, the temptation is to use a long-shanked hook to achieve the correct size. This tactic works well in most instances; however, when fish are proving selective, or when a pattern needs to be dressed sparsely, the weight and stiffness of the large hook can be a problem. The answer lies in a detached body, in which case, rather than being dressed along the hook, the body extends over the bend. This allows a smaller hook to be used, which also reduces weight and helps the fly to float. Various materials may be used to form a detached body, from foam to deer hair. Here the latter is used to create the Detached Body Mayfly.

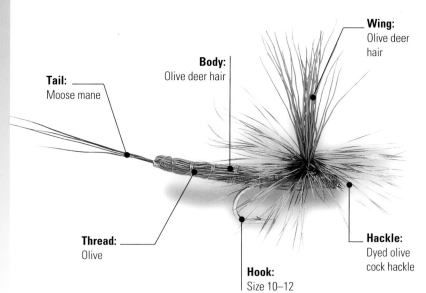

Wing:
Olive deer hair

Body:
Olive deer hair

Tail:
Moose mane

Thread:
Olive

Hook:
Size 10–12

Hackle:
Dyed olive cock hackle

1 Fix a fine sewing needle, point-out, in the vise jaws. Run the tying thread along it in open turns for about 1¼ inches (3cm). At the tail end, catch in a few moose mane hairs, allowing the butts to lie along the needle.

2 Take a pinch of olive deer hair. Trim off the thin, hard tips, making sure that the remaining hairs are undamaged and all the same length. Catch the hair in at the same point as the tail so that the thin ends lie along the needle.

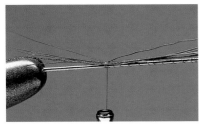

3 Pull the thread tight so the hair flares around the needle. Stroke the deer hair down the length of the needle and wind the thread over it. Use a pattern of tight groups of three, followed by an open turn to merely hold the hair in place.

4 Continue the process to form a body approximately ½-inch (1.5cm) long. Cast off the thread with a whip finish and apply flexible fixative to the hair.

5 While the fixative is drying, place the hook in the vise and run on the thread at the mid-point. Take a bunch of deer hair and catch in the tips. Using thread turns around the base of the hair, bring the wing into an upright position.

6 Take the thread to the bend, then slide the open ends of the detached body along the shank and secure with groups of thread turns along the body. Trim off the excess hair before adding an olive cock hackle in the parachute style.

Cutwing Caddis

Brown trout

Cutthroat

Rainbow trout

Caddis flies make up a high proportion of the trout's diet in both rivers and natural lakes. A warm summer's evening is the best time to find fish taking the freshly emerged adults as they skitter across the water's surface, and is also the most effective time to use a well-tied imitation. An adult caddis fly imitation needs to be retrieved to imitate the action of the natural, so it is important to tie it with buoyant materials that won't easily become waterlogged. The Cutwing Caddis fulfills this criterion by having a body and thorax made from dubbed deer hair, the natural buoyancy of which helps it to float. The lifelike profile of this fly comes from the wing, created by gluing a hackle feather to a sheet of fine nylon mesh. When dry, the feather may be cut to the typical caddis fly shape.

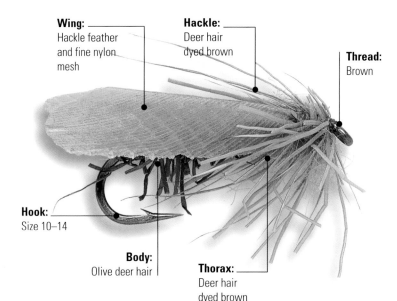

Wing:
Hackle feather and fine nylon mesh

Hackle:
Deer hair dyed brown

Thread:
Brown

Hook:
Size 10–14

Body:
Olive deer hair

Thorax:
Deer hair dyed brown

90

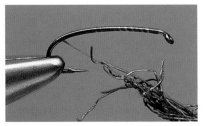

1 Once the hook is fixed in the vise, run the tying thread from the eye to a point opposite the barb. Tear rather than cut a pinch of olive deer hair from the skin and apply it to the tying thread.

2 Using the standard finger-and-thumb twist, dub the deer hair onto the tying thread. If this proves difficult, apply a sticky wax to the thread first. Start to wind the dubbed hair along the shank.

3 Cover two-thirds of the hook with the dubbed deer hair, aiming to form a relatively fat body.

4 Select a pre-prepared wing that has been cut to the shape of a caddis fly wing. These are formed by gluing a hackle feather to a fine nylon mesh before cutting to the required shape.

5 Press the wing so that it folds along its central rib, then catch it in position at the eye so that it wraps around the sides of the body.

6 Tear a pinch of dyed brown deer hair and place it in a dubbing loop. Spin the loop before winding the hair on as a combined thorax and hackle. Twist a few fibers to give the impression of leg joints. Cast off the thread.

91

CHAPTER TWO

NYMPHS
AND
BUGS

Where dry flies imitate all those creatures to be found on the water's surface, nymphs and bugs provide the subsurface equivalent. Patterns that fall within this category include those that either suggest or directly imitate the nymphs and larvae of all the main aquatic fly groups, including mayflies, stoneflies, caddis flies, and midges, plus the smaller species of freshwater crustaceans. However, many nymph patterns are tied simply to provide an impression of something alive and edible. Interestingly, this latter group includes many of the most successful of all nymphs, patterns such as the Hare's Ear Nymph, the Pheasant Tail Nymph, and the Fox Squirrel Nymph.

The vast majority of the trout's prey is found among the weeds and stones on river bottoms. For this reason, many nymphs and bugs are weighted so that they sink quickly to the fish's feeding level. To accomplish this sink rate, additional weight can be added to a heavy-wire hook by using materials such as lead wire, lead foil, or metal beads. Metal beads come

in a range of colors, including gold, silver, and copper, and are usually fixed at the eye or bend, so they are visible and add some sparkle. Conversely, the more somber-colored lead wire and foil is normally applied directly to the hook so that it remains hidden under the fly's body materials. By concealing the weight under the dressing, imitations of creatures, such as caddis larvae and scuds, can be tied with plenty of weight while still looking lifelike enough to fool the fish.

Hare's Ear Nymph

Brown trout

Cutthroat

Grayling

Rainbow trout

Sea trout

This is the classic all-purpose nymph, effective for many game fish species in all water types and conditions. The key to its success is the mottled brown hues of the hare's fur that can suggest all manner of small aquatic insect larvae or crustaceans. It can also be tied in a whole range of sizes from a big, heavy size 8 longshank right down to a 22—truly a most versatile pattern. When using hare's fur, the effect can be varied depending on the amount of underfur and guard hairs used. The more guard hairs, the rougher and spikier the finished fly. Teasing out the hair once the fly has been tied will enhance the texture. This can be done with either the tip of a needle or, better still, a piece of Velcro.

Body:
Hare's fur

Wing cases:
Gray feather fiber

Tail:
Hare's guard hairs

Thread:
Brown

Hook:
Size 8–22

Rib:
Fine gold tinsel

Weight:
Lead wire

1 Secure the hook in the vise. Wind on four turns of lead wire behind the eye and cover them with tying thread. Catch in a few fibers of hare's fur as a tail plus 2 inches (5cm) of fine, gold tinsel.

2 Cover the waste ends of the hair and tinsel with thread before dubbing on a body of hare's fur. This should be a mix of guard hairs and softer underfur. Wind the hare's fur right up to the turns of lead wire.

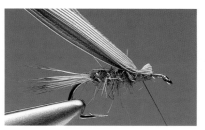

3 Take hold of the gold tinsel and wind it over the fur in the opposite direction. This will prevent it bedding in. Secure the loose end of the tinsel with thread and remove the excess.

4 Take a slip of gray feather fiber and catch it in by its tip, where the body ends.

5 Dub on a second, smaller pinch of hare's fur, again with a blend of stiffer guard hairs and softer underfur. Wind it over the lead wire to form the thorax.

6 Pull the gray feather fibers over the top of the thorax and secure at the eye. Remove the excess feather, then build a neat head. Cast off.

Flashback Pheasant Tail Nymph

This pattern is a variation of the classic Pheasant Tail Nymph. Its body, tail, and rib are the same as the original, but the thorax of this pattern includes a few strands of pearl Lurex laid over the peacock herl. Pearl Lurex gives a wonderful flash and sparkle to any fly, and in the case of the Flashback Pheasant Tail Nymph only a small amount of the material is used to keep the effect as subtle as possible. The aim is to suggest the sparkle caused by gases trapped within the skin of a mature nymph as it rises to the surface to transform into the winged dun. This pattern is highly effective on both rivers and lakes, especially during a hatch of small- to medium-sized dark mayflies.

Brown trout

Cutthroat

Grayling

Rainbow trout

Rib:
Fine copper wire

Tail:
Cock pheasant tail fibers

Body:
Cock pheasant tail fibers

Thorax Cover:
Pearl Lurex

Hook:
Size 12–20

Thorax:
Peacock herl

Thread:
Black

96

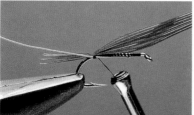  

1 Fix the hook and run the tying thread down the shank to a point opposite the barb. Catch in four or five male pheasant tail fibers, allowing the tips to project past the bend. At the same point, catch in 2 inches (5cm) of fine, copper wire.

2 Wind the thread two-thirds of the way back up the shank. Then, holding the butts of the pheasant tail fibers, wind them over the hook so that they cover two-thirds of its length.

3 Secure the loose ends of the pheasant tail fibers with thread turns. Next, take hold of the copper wire and wind it over the pheasant tail in open, evenly spaced turns. This rib protects the delicate feather fibers.

4 Using the loose end of the copper wire, build a thorax base with close turns before securing and removing the excess wire and pheasant tail. Just in front of the body, catch in two strands of pearl Lurex.

5 At the same point as the pearl Lurex, catch in two strands of peacock herl by their tips. Twist the fibers together gently and wind them over the close turns of copper wire to form the thorax.

6 Secure the loose ends of the peacock herl at the eye and remove the excess. Finally, draw the pearl Lurex over the back of the thorax and secure at the eye. Remove the excess Lurex, build a neat head, and cast off the thread.

97

Teeny Nymph

Developed by top American fly fisher Jim Teeny, the Teeny
Nymph is a simple but deadly pattern. It is tied in a wide range
of sizes and colors and is effective for most species of game fish.
The body material is comprised of cock pheasant tail fibers,
either plain brown or dyed a range of colors, such as black,
purple, pink, orange, and olive. The Teeny Nymph is quick and
easy to tie so is a great pattern for fishing rocky ground where
flies are all too readily snagged and lost. Without fearing the loss
of an expensive fly, the angler can confidently work even the
toughest fish-holding areas, where the bigger fish lie.

Brown
trout

Rainbow
trout

Coho
salmon

Steelhead

Chinook
salmon

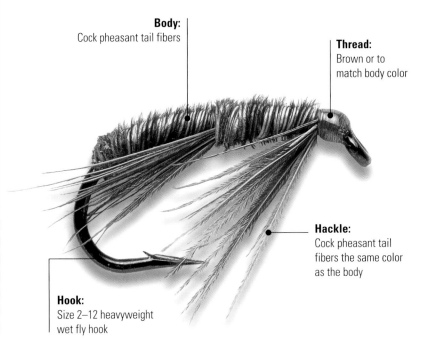

Body:
Cock pheasant tail fibers

Thread:
Brown or to
match body color

Hackle:
Cock pheasant tail
fibers the same color
as the body

Hook:
Size 2–12 heavyweight
wet fly hook

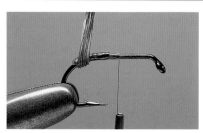

1 With the hook fixed in the vise, run the tying thread on at the eye and carry it down the shank and slightly around the bend. Take 10 or more cock pheasant tail fibers and catch them in by their butts.

2 Wind the thread halfway down the shank and apply a drop of clear lacquer. Leave until tacky. Wind the pheasant tail fibers along the hook so that they also cover half the shank length.

3 Make sure that the fibers lie flat and are not twisted, then secure the tips with tight thread wraps.

4 Fold the tips of the fibers back and beneath the hook so that they form a hackle. Secure them in place with turns of tying thread.

5 Take a second bunch of pheasant tail fibers, this one slightly longer than the first. Catch it in just in front of the rear body section. Apply another drop of lacquer to the thread used to catch in the fibers.

6 Wind the fibers up to the eye and secure with thread. Fold back and beneath the hook as with the previous bunch to form another hackle. Cast off the thread.

99

Red Fox Squirrel Nymph

Brown trout

Cutthroat

Rainbow trout

Dave Whitlock developed this fine general nymph pattern. It uses the various colors and textures of hair on the red fox squirrel for almost every part of its construction. It is a robust and easy-to-tie pattern, the only possible problem coming from dubbing the stiff guard hairs used for the thorax. To solve this, once the hairs have been removed from the skin they should be rubbed around in the palm of the hand to mix the direction in which they lie. This helps produce a more homogenous dubbing where the softer underfur holds the spiky guard hairs in place. Also, using plenty of wax on the tying thread will help the hair to stick.

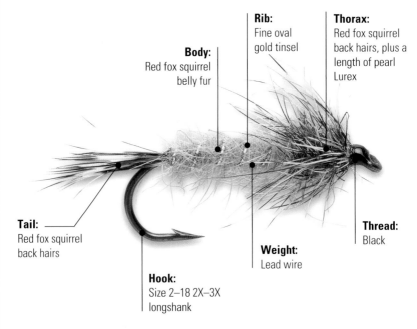

Rib:
Fine oval gold tinsel

Thorax:
Red fox squirrel back hairs, plus a length of pearl Lurex

Body:
Red fox squirrel belly fur

Tail:
Red fox squirrel back hairs

Hook:
Size 2–18 2X–3X longshank

Weight:
Lead wire

Thread:
Black

1 Fix the hook and wind on close turns of lead wire, starting just short of the eye. Leave a section of the hook shank bare at the bend. Secure the wire with wraps of tying thread. Take a pinch of red fox squirrel back hairs and tie in as a tail.

2 Take 2 inches (5cm) of fine, oval, gold tinsel and secure it in place at the base of the tail. Leave the waste end short so that it helps fill the bare section of hook to the rear of the lead wire.

3 Tease out a generous pinch of the red fox squirrel belly fur. Apply it to the tying thread, which should be well waxed. Dub it onto the thread with a simple finger-and-thumb twist and start to wind it over the lead underbody.

4 Make sure the body material is closely wound and that it tapers slightly to the rear. Stop at the start of the lead underbody. Wind on gold tinsel in six turns to cover the length of the shank. Secure the loose end and remove the excess.

5 Fold a length of pearl Lurex in half and catch it in at the front of the body.

6 Trim the Lurex to two short stubs. Wax the tying thread again and apply a pinch of spiky back hairs from a fox squirrel. Dub them on to form a thick rope and wind up to the eye to form the thorax. Complete with a neat head and cast off.

Brassie

Small, simple, and deadly is the best way to describe the Brassie. It uses just two materials in its construction to form an effective imitation of a wide range of midge pupae. Being simple, it can be tied very small—right down to a size 20 hook. The most important part of the fly is the body, formed by close turns of wire that create a slim profile and add extra weight. This wire body helps the Brassie to sink quickly, making it an ideal subsurface pattern for use on rivers and lakes. In the original Brassie, copper electrical wire was used for the body, but with the introduction of colored wires a much greater range of effects can be created. While body color can vary, the thorax is normally peacock herl or a dark dubbing such as muskrat or rabbit fur.

Brown
trout

Cutthroat

Grayling

Rainbow
trout

Thorax:
Muskrat or dark rabbit fur

Body:
Fine copper
wire

Thread:
Black

Hook:
Size 12–20

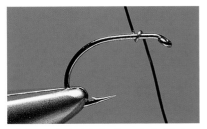

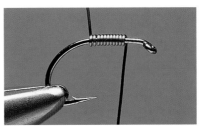

1 Secure the hook in the vise and take 3 inches (7.5cm) of fine, copper wire. Holding both ends of the wire make one forward turn.

2 Using the leading end, wind the wire toward the eye in touching turns, making sure that no gaps form.

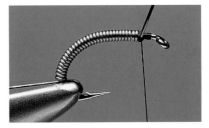

3 When a dozen or so turns have been made, trim off the end to the rear with scissors. If a sharp end sticks up, pinch it down with pliers.

4 Slide the turns a little around the bend and wind on more turns, working along the shank toward the eye. Keep winding the wire and sliding the turns well around the bend until the whole shank is covered.

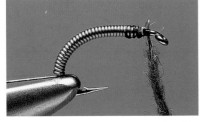

5 Secure the loose end of the copper wire with tying thread and remove the excess. Take a pinch of muskrat, or dark rabbit fur, and dub it onto the tying thread to form a fluffy rope.

6 Wind the dubbed fur toward the eye to form a pronounced thorax. Build a small, neat head at the eye and cast off the thread as usual.

Serendipity

The Serendipity has a buoyant thorax constructed from deer hair, which has been spun and clipped into shape, and is a very effective imitation of a midge pupa. When chironomid midge pupae transpose into adults, they must first rise to the water's surface, hanging with the back of the thorax right in the surface film. This critical stage in the insect's life is mimicked beautifully by the Serendipity. The technique used to form the thorax is the same as used for a standard Muddler head, only the scale is different. When first tying this pattern, it is a good idea to apply the deer hair in two stages, first the collar, then a second bunch taken right up to the eye. With practice, the hair can eventually be applied in one bunch.

Brown trout

Arctic char

Cutthroat

Grayling

Rainbow trout

Atlantic salmon

Sea trout

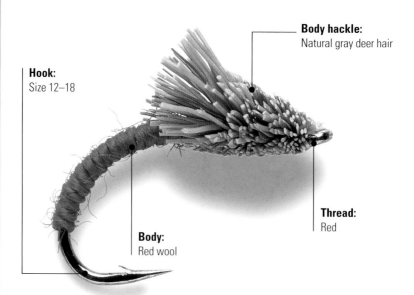

Body hackle:
Natural gray deer hair

Hook:
Size 12–18

Thread:
Red

Body:
Red wool

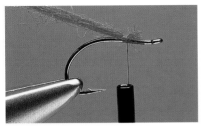

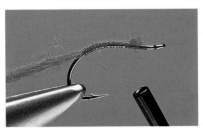

1 Having fixed the hook in the vise, run the tying thread on at the eye and carry it a short distance down the shank. Take a thin strand of red wool and catch it in just behind the eye.

2 Wind the thread over the wool in close turns, taking it well around the bend of the hook. This will form an even base for the wool body.

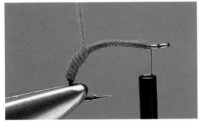

3 Gently twist the wool so that it becomes very thin and tight. Wind this in touching turns back around the shank to form a slim body with a noticeable ribbed effect.

4 Secure the wool with thread and remove the excess. Take a small bunch of deer hair, offer it up to the hook, and wind two loose turns of thread over it.

5 Begin to pull the thread tight, adding further, tighter turns. This will cause the deer hair to flare around the hook and form the base for the head.

6 Push the hair back and fix with thread. Repeat the process, adding hair so that it reaches the eye. Cast off the thread, then trim the head to shape with scissors.

105

Suspender Buzzer

Brown trout

Rainbow trout

Plastic microcellular foam is one of the great successes of modern fly-tying. Being buoyant and extremely tough, it is perfect for creating a whole range of dry flies and emerger patterns. The key to using foam is judging the amount needed—as little as possible, so that the fly still floats but bulk is kept to a minimum. In this pattern, a small strip of foam is folded over to form a buoyant thorax. In this way, the Suspender Buzzer, which imitates a small, hatching midge, sits with only its thorax floating in the surface film, just like the real thing. Here, white foam colored with a permanent marker has been used, but other colored foams work equally well.

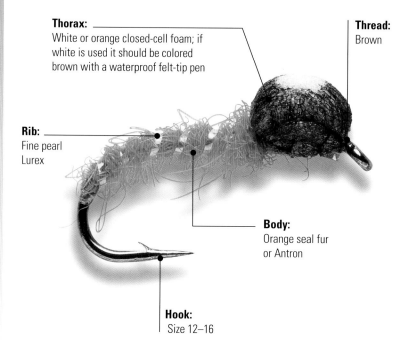

Thorax:
White or orange closed-cell foam; if white is used it should be colored brown with a waterproof felt-tip pen

Thread:
Brown

Rib:
Fine pearl Lurex

Body:
Orange seal fur or Antron

Hook:
Size 12–16

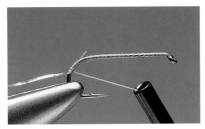

1 Fix the hook in the vise and run on the tying thread. Carry the thread around the hook bend and catch in 2 inches (5cm) of fine, pearl Lurex.

2 Take a pinch of orange seal fur and offer it up to waxed tying thread. Dub the fur to form a thin rope and start to wind it along the hook shank.

3 Stop the fur two-thirds of the way toward the eye. The aim is to create a slim, tapered body. Wind the Lurex over the fur in evenly spaced turns. Secure and remove the excess Lurex.

4 From a sheet of foam, cut a strip 2 inches (5cm) long and ¼ inch (0.5cm) wide. Catch it in so that the waste end runs from the eye to the start of the body. Secure the waste end with thread.

5 Fold the foam gently back to the eye. Don't stretch it tight as this will flatten the foam and reduce its buoyancy. To secure, use loose thread wraps that won't compress the foam.

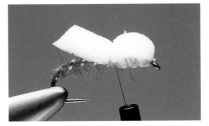

6 With the tying thread positioned in front of the body, fold the foam back again and secure in one place. Cast off the thread, trim off the waste foam, and color with a felt-tip pen.

107

Egg Fly

Arctic char

Cutthroat

Grayling

Rainbow trout

Atlantic salmon

The Egg Fly is tied to represent a salmon egg—a source of food for many species of fish, including rainbow trout, char, and grayling. When Pacific salmon are on their reds, the number of eggs laid is simply vast, and other fish will congregate behind the spawning fish and pick off any eggs that drift downstream. The pattern is extremely simple to tie, the procedure being similar to that used for applying deer hair. First, a short, thick bunch of Glo-bug yarn is tied to the middle of the hook with very strong thread. This thread is pulled tight so that it digs deep into the yarn. The yarn is then pulled tight above the hook and trimmed short with a single, curved cut. The result is a round fish-egg shape. Various colors of yarn can be used, including pink, peach, and orange. Some Egg Flies use more than one color in their construction, with a contrasting spot at the top.

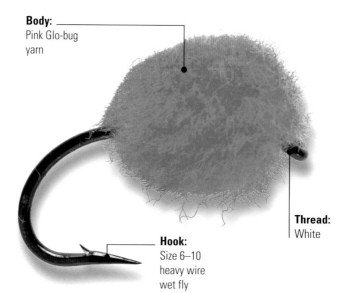

Body:
Pink Glo-bug
yarn

Thread:
White

Hook:
Size 6–10
heavy wire
wet fly

1 Having fixed the hook in the vise, run on the very strong tying thread midway along the shank. Catch in place a short section of pink Glo-bug yarn halfway along its length.

2 Add further strands of yarn on both sides of the first, fixing them in place with tight turns of thread.

3 If required, a final strand of yarn in a contrasting color can be applied on top of the others. This will produce a bright spot in the finished fly.

4 Pull the yarn up and wind tight turns of thread around its base to finally secure it to the hook. Cast off the thread at this point.

5 Trim the yarn short with single scissor cuts. This cut should be slightly curved toward both ends to help create the egg shape.

6 As the cut fibers spring back, they will fall naturally into a rough egg shape. Use small cuts to tidy the shape and ensure a nice round profile.

Rabbit Fly

Brown trout

Rainbow trout

When tying flies exclusively for use on lakes, it pays to have as much built-in action as possible. The Rabbit Fly fulfills this criterion by having a collar and tail of soft rabbit fur that moves well in the water, even when the fly is retrieved very slowly. Although tied as a general nymph pattern, the Rabbit Fly makes a pretty good imitation of the small dragonfly nymphs that emerge in huge numbers on many Australian lakes. Tied with just a few turns of lead wire under the body, the pattern should be cast close to any drowned timber or other obstructions—just where the trout patrol on the lookout for real dragonfly nymphs.

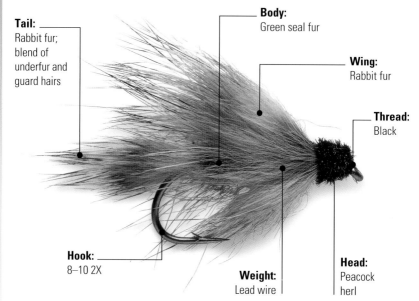

Tail:
Rabbit fur; blend of underfur and guard hairs

Body:
Green seal fur

Wing:
Rabbit fur

Thread:
Black

Hook:
8–10 2X

Weight:
Lead wire

Head:
Peacock herl

1 Wind on close turns of lead wire to opposite the hook point and secure in place with tying thread. Select a pinch of rabbit fur that contains a blend of soft underfur and the stiffer guard hairs. Catch it in behind the lead wire.

2 Apply a pinch of green seal fur to the tying thread and dub it on with a simple finger-and-thumb twist.

3 Wind the dubbed fur over the lead wire underbody in close turns. Take a second pinch of rabbit fur, slightly longer than the distance between the eye and the tail tip. Catch it in so that it projects over the eye.

4 Making sure that the rabbit fur has flared evenly around the hook, stroke it back over the body and fix in position with tight thread turns.

5 Take two strands of peacock herl and catch them in, by their tips, at the eye.

6 Twist the herls together gently to form a rope. Wind this over the base of the wing to form the head. Cast off the thread and run on a drop of clear lacquer to fix the herls.

111

Brown
trout

Arctic
char

Cutthroat

Grayling

Rainbow
trout

Goldhead Bug

This is more a generic style of tying than an individual pattern. Goldhead Bugs can be tied in a variety of colors, although they all have a metal gold bead at the head to give weight and a fish-attracting sparkle. Being well weighted, Goldhead Bugs are designed to fish deep, and they work well both in lakes and rivers. When using a gold bead, it is important to find a hook that will accept it. The shape of some hooks prevents the bead slipping around the bend, so it is always worth checking first. For most patterns, an ordinary gold bead plus turns of lead wire provide enough weight, but it is now possible to buy tungsten beads, which are even heavier and sink faster.

Rib:
Fine oval
gold tinsel

Body:
Amber, cream, olive,
or brown fur

Head:
Gold bead

Thread:
Brown

Tail:
Pearl Crystal
Hair, cut short

Underbody:
Lead wire

Thorax:
Orange or red fur

Hook:
Size 10–14

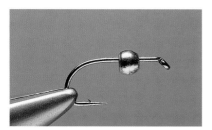

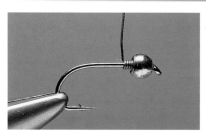

1 Select a hook that will accommodate the gold bead. Before fixing the hook in the vise, slip the gold bead over the point and slide it to the eye. Secure the hook in the vise.

2 With the bead tight against the eye of the hook, wind on a few turns of lead wire, pushing them into the recess at the back of the bead.

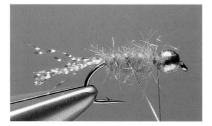

3 Run on the tying thread, using it to fix the lead wire in place. Carry the thread down the shank and catch in a few strands of pearl Crystal Hair opposite the barb.

4 Catch in 2 inches (5cm) of fine, oval, gold tinsel at the base of the tail and dub on a generous pinch of amber fur. Wind the dubbed fur up to the bead. The finished body should be quite chunky, mimicking the shape of a caddis pupa.

5 Wind on the oval, gold tinsel, making three evenly spaced turns. Secure with thread and remove the excess.

6 Dub on a pinch of orange fur and wind it on as a collar. Cast off the thread with a whip finish and trim the Crystal Hair tail to length.

113

Peeping Caddis

This ingenious pattern imitates a cased caddis larva as it crawls along the riverbed. As a caddis larva moves, its legs, plus the front part of its body, peep out of the front of the case. The Peeping Caddis uses a short section of yarn with brown partridge feather to imitate this, and by burning the tip of the yarn with a match flame it is possible to mimic the larva's dark head. As the pattern is designed to fish right on the bottom, it is heavily weighted with turns of lead wire, along with a metal bead at the eye. Dubbing on a large pinch of hare or squirrel fur forms the caddis's case. The proportion of the stiffer guard hairs used will alter how rough the effect is.

Brown trout

Cutthroat

Grayling

Rainbow trout

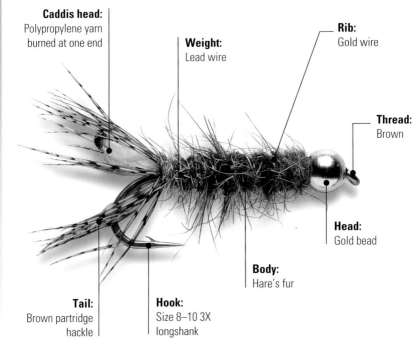

Caddis head:
Polypropylene yarn burned at one end

Weight:
Lead wire

Rib:
Gold wire

Thread:
Brown

Head:
Gold bead

Body:
Hare's fur

Tail:
Brown partridge hackle

Hook:
Size 8–10 3X longshank

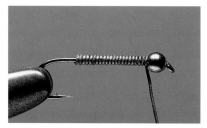

1 Select a hook that will accommodate the gold bead, and slip it over the point and up to the eye before fixing the hook in the vise. Wind on close turns of lead wire. Leave a small gap in the wire underbody, toward the bend of the hook.

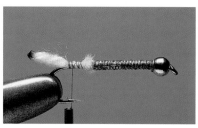

2 Run on the tying thread at the eye and wind it over the lead wire. Catch in a short length of yarn, burned at one end, at the bend, in the gap left behind the lead body.

3 Prepare a brown partridge hackle, stroking the fibers away from the tip. Catch it in by its tip, at the base of the yarn body.

4 Hold the hackle by the base with hackle pliers and wind on three turns. Stroke the fibers back after each turn so that they project over the yarn. Secure the hackle and trim off the excess.

5 Catch in 3 inches (7.5cm) of fine, gold wire before applying a body of dubbed hare's fur.

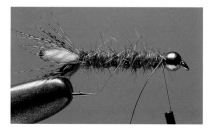

6 Carry the hare's fur right up to the bead, then wind evenly spaced turns of the gold wire to form the rib. Secure the wire and remove the excess. Cast off the tying thread.

115

Sparkle Pupa

A comprehensive study of the caddis fly's life cycle gave Gary LaFontaine the inspiration for this superbly designed imitation. It is tied to imitate a caddis pupa as it emerges to transpose into the winged adult. What makes it so clever is LaFontaine's use of Antron tied as a loose envelope over the main body. The result is that air trapped within the fibers produces a sparkle similar to that formed by gases within the skin of the natural. It is a pattern that works well on both rivers and lakes, wherever trout or grayling are taking caddis pupae. It is tied in both ginger, as this version, or gray. Hook size ranges from 10 to 18.

Brown trout

Cutthroat

Grayling

Rainbow trout

Wing:
Brown elk hair

Tail:
Clear Antron yarn

Head:
Beige dubbing

Hook:
Size 10–18

Body envelope:
Amber Antron yarn

Underbody:
Equal mix of ginger dubbing fur and amber Antron

Thread:
Brown

1 With the hook fixed in the vise, run the tying thread down the shank in touching turns. Stop at a point just opposite the barb and catch in a small bunch of clear Antron as a shuck.

2 Take a strand of amber Antron and divide it, lengthwise, in two. Catch one half above and one half below the hook shank. Cover the waste ends with a few wraps of thread.

3 Offer a pinch of ginger fur and amber Antron up to the tying thread. Dub the blend onto the thread with a finger-and-thumb twist and wind it along the shank to form a chunky body.

4 With the tying thread situated just behind the eye, pull the top strand of the Antron yarn loosely over the back of the body. Secure with the tying thread.

5 Repeat the process with the yarn below the hook shank. Again, keep it loose. The aim is to create an envelope that will hold air bubbles.

6 Remove the excess amber Antron. Trim the tail to length, then add a short wing of elk hair in front of the body. Complete with a head of beige dubbing, casting off the thread with a whip finish.

Timberline Emerger

This brilliant little pattern was designed by top U.S. angler Randal Kaufman, and is deadly when trout are taking small, emerging mayflies. Tied on a light wire hook the pattern can be fished dead-drift just under the surface, and is a great fly to try when trout are rising steadily but ordinary dun imitations are being refused. The immature wings of the natural are imitated by using two grizzle hackle points tied short, while a slim tail of gray marabou gives the impression of the nymph's shed skin. The Timberline Emerger works best in smaller sizes, from a size 14 hook down to a size 22.

Brown trout

Cutthroat

Rainbow trout

Wing:
Grizzle hackle points tied short

Body:
Gray muskrat and seal fur blended together

Thread:
Gray

Tail:
Gray marabou

Hook:
Size 14–22

Hackle:
Brown cock hackle

Rib:
Fine gold wire

1 Once the hook is fixed in the vise, wind the tying thread down the shank from the eye to a point opposite the barb. Catch in a pinch of gray marabou along with 2 inches (5cm) of fine, gold wire.

2 Cover the waste ends with thread, forming an even base for the body. Return the thread to the bend and dub on a small pinch of gray fur. Wind the dubbed fur back along the shank, in close turns, stopping just short of the eye.

3 Take hold of the gold wire and wind it over the body in evenly spaced turns. Secure the end and remove the excess.

4 Take two grizzle hackle points and place them together, dull-sides in. Remove the fibers from the stalks to leave two short tips. Catch in at the eye.

5 Fold over the bare stalks and secure with thread. Remove the excess. Prepare a brown cock hackle and catch it in just in front of the wing.

6 Take hold of the hackle with hackle pliers and wind on two turns in front of the wing. Secure the loose end with thread and remove the excess. Build a small, neat head and cast off.

Baetis Nymph

This is a very effective imitation of a range of small mayfly. Being lightly dressed, it is usually fished quite near the surface, mimicking a nymph on its way to transposing into the winged dun. The body is tied in various shades of olive and gray, and partridge feather fibers are used for both the tail and to imitate the insect's legs. Allowed to dead-drift with the current, a gentle lift of the rod top causes the nymph to rise in the water and often triggers a positive response from the fish. The Baetis Nymph works in a range of hook sizes from a size 12 down to a size 20, depending on the species hatching.

Brown trout

Cutthroat

Grayling

Rainbow trout

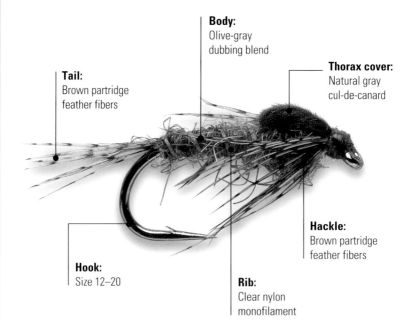

Body:
Olive-gray
dubbing blend

Thorax cover:
Natural gray
cul-de-canard

Tail:
Brown partridge
feather fibers

Hackle:
Brown partridge
feather fibers

Hook:
Size 12–20

Rib:
Clear nylon
monofilament

1 Having fixed the hook in the vise, run the tying thread to a point opposite the barb. Catch in a few fibers of brown partridge feather as a tail and 2 inches (5cm) of fine, clear nylon. Dub a pinch of olive-gray fur onto the thread.

2 Gently twist the fur to form a thin rope, then wind it along the shank in close turns so that it forms a slim, slightly tapered body.

3 Wind the clear nylon over the body in the opposite spiral to the fur. This produces a fine, segmented effect. Secure the loose end of the nylon with thread and remove the excess.

4 Take two natural gray cul-de-canard feathers and catch them in by their tips in front of the body.

5 Dub on a second smaller pinch of olive-gray fur and wind it on to form the thorax. Take a few fibers of brown partridge feather and catch in as a beard hackle.

6 Pull the cul-de-canard feathers over the thorax and secure them at the eye. Trim off the excess feathers, build a small head, and cast off the thread with a whip finish.

Woolly Worm

Heavy and big, the Woolly Worm is a great "bottom grubbing" pattern for both rivers and lakes. Close turns of lead wire are used to give the weight, while chenille produces a chunky body. A grizzle cock hackle is wound the length of the body so the pattern has plenty of life; and, when tied in various colors, it can be used to suggest anything from a caddis larva to a stonefly nymph. The Woolly Worm is tied on a longshank hook, so long, genetic saddle hackles are normally used. These have the size plus the consistent fiber length to allow them to be wound the entire length of a large hook.

Brown trout

Cutthroat

Rainbow trout

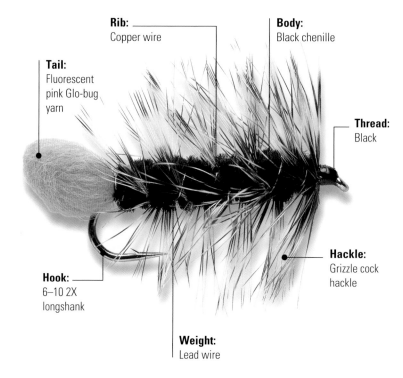

Rib:
Copper wire

Body:
Black chenille

Tail:
Fluorescent pink Glo-bug yarn

Thread:
Black

Hackle:
Grizzle cock hackle

Hook:
6–10 2X longshank

Weight:
Lead wire

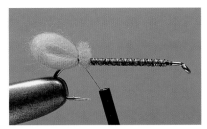

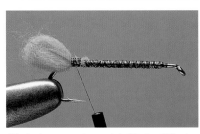

1 Fix the hook in the vise. Starting by the eye, wind on turns of lead wire to opposite the hook point. Run on the tying thread at the eye and wind it closely over the lead wire. Catch in a loop of Glo-bug yarn at the bend, behind the lead body.

2 At the same point, catch in 3 inches (7.5cm) of copper wire. This will form the rib.

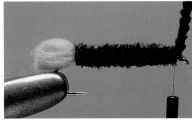

3 Remove some of the fibers from the end of a 4-inch (10-cm) length of black chenille to expose its core. Catch in the chenille using the bare section. Wind it over the lead wire to the eye using touching turns. Secure and remove the waste end.

4 Select a soft-fibered grizzle cock hackle and catch it in at the eye.

5 Grasp the tip of the hackle with a pair of hackle pliers. Wind it down the shank in evenly spaced turns, carrying the hackle right to the tail.

6 Wind the copper wire to the eye in evenly spaced turns. This locks the hackle in place. Remove the excess wire and hackle tips, and build a small head before casting off.

Montana Nymph

This pattern was originally designed as a simple-to-tie imitation of a variety of large, dark stonefly nymphs. It has since become widely used as a general nymph pattern, particularly on lakes. Apart from the tail and hackle, the main component of the Montana Nymph is chenille. The original combination was black and yellow but, especially in the United Kingdom, fluorescent lime-green has been substituted for the latter. Like most patterns that incorporate chenille, care must be taken to prevent unsightly bumps from forming. Being bulky, the fibers of chenille should be stripped from a short section of the core and this much thinner core caught in with the tying thread.

Brown trout

Cutthroat

Rainbow trout

Tail:
Black cock hackle fibers

Body:
Black chenille

Thorax:
Fluorescent lime-green chenille

Thorax cover:
Black chenille

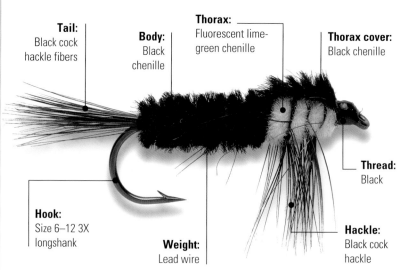

Thread:
Black

Hook:
Size 6–12 3X longshank

Weight:
Lead wire

Hackle:
Black cock hackle

1 Fix the hook and, starting just short of the eye, wind on turns of lead wire to form a weighted underbody. Stop opposite the hook point. Run on the tying thread at the eye and wind it closely over the lead wire. Catch in a few black hackle fibers.

2 Remove some of the fibers from the end of a 3-inch (7.5-cm) length of black chenille to expose the core. Catch the chenille in by the core, then wind it along the shank. When the body is formed, secure the chenille and remove the excess.

3 In front of the body, catch in a second length of black chenille, 2 inches (5cm) of fluorescent lime-green chenille, and a dyed black cock hackle.

4 Take hold of the lime-green chenille, either with the fingers or a pair of hackle pliers— these stop the chenille from being damaged— and wind it up to the eye. Secure and remove the excess.

5 Take hold of the hackle tip with hackle pliers and wind on three evenly spaced turns. Allow the turns of hackle to bed between the turns of chenille. Secure the hackle tip and remove the excess.

6 Pull the black chenille over the back of the thorax and secure at the eye. Trim the waste end. Build a neat head and cast off the thread.

Palomino Midge

Detached-bodied flies are becoming increasingly popular because they allow a small, light hook to be used. In the Palomino Midge, a very fine, tough chenille, known as vernille, is used to create the abdomen of the chironomid midge pupa. The vernille helps create an extremely natural effect; by exposing a short section of the core, at the tail, the white breathing filaments are represented. The Palomino Midge is tied in a range of body colors from black and brown to olive and red. In each, though, the thorax is the same, comprising either peacock herl or a dark fur, such as muskrat. The pattern is tied on a short-shank hook ranging in size from a 14 to an 18.

Brown trout

Cutthroat

Rainbow trout

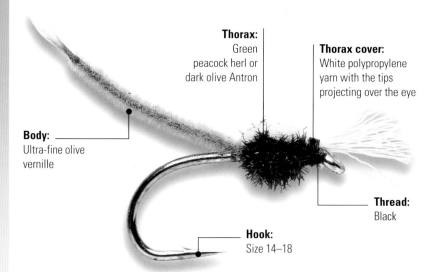

Thorax:
Green peacock herl or dark olive Antron

Thorax cover:
White polypropylene yarn with the tips projecting over the eye

Body:
Ultra-fine olive vernille

Thread:
Black

Hook:
Size 14–18

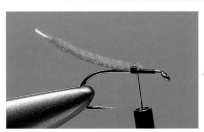

1 Once the hook is fixed in the vise, run the tying thread on at the eye and carry it almost halfway along the shank. Take a short length of olive, ultra-fine vernille.

2 Remove the flue to expose a small amount of the core. This will represent the breathing filaments of the midge. Secure the vernille in position with thread wraps.

3 With the detached body in place, take approximately 1 inch (2.5cm) of white polypropylene yarn. Catch it in so that the yarn lies over the body.

4 Take two strands of green peacock herl and catch them in by their tips, just in front of the polypropylene yarn. Take the tying thread down to the eye.

5 Gently twist the peacock herl strands together so that they form a fluffy rope. Wind this up to the eye to form a pronounced thorax.

6 Secure the herls and remove the excess. Pull the yarn over the back of the thorax and fix at the eye with thread. Cast off the thread and trim the yarn to form short breathers.

127

Bloodworm

Brown
trout

Rainbow
trout

In lakes and slower-moving rivers, the larvae of the chironomid midge make up a large part of the trout's diet. They vary in color from pale green and brown to a bright blood red. These red larvae, known by anglers as bloodworm, live the bulk of their lives in silt tubes, but when disturbed or migrating can move by a sinuous lashing motion. This action is almost impossible to replicate, but by adding a small pinch of red marabou as a tail, enough action can be imparted to make an effective imitation. The remainder of the fly is simply translucent red Nymph Glass, which is wound in touching turns along the hook.

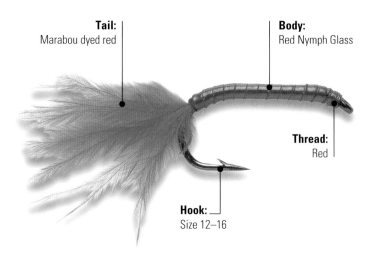

Tail:
Marabou dyed red

Body:
Red Nymph Glass

Thread:
Red

Hook:
Size 12–16

1 Fix the hook in the vise and run the tying thread down the shank, stopping a short distance around the bend. Take a pinch of dyed red marabou and catch it in place at this point.

2 Wind close turns of thread over the waste ends of the marabou. This will form an even base for the body and ensure a smooth finish.

3 Once the eye has been reached, take 4 inches (10cm) of red Nymph Glass and catch it in with three tight thread wraps.

4 Stretch the Nymph Glass and secure it along the length of the shank with closely wound turns of tying thread.

5 When the tail is reached, take the thread back to the eye. Wind the Nymph Glass around the shank to the eye in tight, closely butted turns. Keep a steady tension at all times.

6 Secure the loose end with tying thread and remove the excess Nymph Glass. Build a neat head and cast off the tying thread.

Prince Nymph

Brown
trout

Arctic
char

Rainbow
trout

Though it has the overall profile of a stonefly nymph, the Prince
Nymph is a great general nymph pattern, effective on both rivers
and lakes. Its body is formed using the standard technique of
winding twisted strands of peacock herl over turns of lead wire,
which creates a chunky effect. The tail and wing are formed
from goose biots—brown for the tail and white for the wing.
These biots come from the "bad" side of a goose primary
feather, and are so stiff and lacking in any flue that they are
unusable for almost anything else. The Prince Nymph also works
well tied with a gold bead at the head.

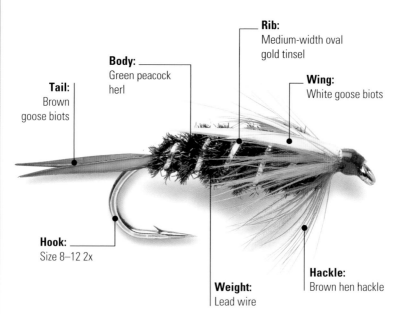

Rib:
Medium-width oval
gold tinsel

Body:
Green peacock
herl

Wing:
White goose biots

Tail:
Brown
goose biots

Hook:
Size 8–12 2x

Weight:
Lead wire

Hackle:
Brown hen hackle

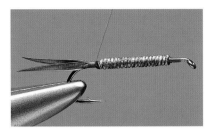

1 Fix the hook in the vise and wind on close turns of lead wire, leaving a short bare section of shank to the front and rear, to form a weighted underbody. Secure the wire with thread and catch in two brown goose biots as the tail.

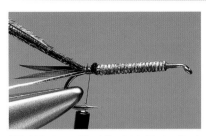

2 At the base of the tail, catch in 2 inches (5cm) of medium-width, oval, gold tinsel and three or four strands of green peacock herl.

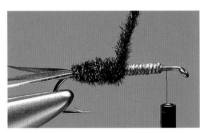

3 Wind the thread up the shank, stopping just short of the eye. Gently twist the strands of peacock herl to form a fluffy rope before winding them over the lead underbody.

4 Secure the loose ends of the herl, remove the waste, and wind on evenly spaced turns of the tinsel to form the rib. Secure the tinsel and remove the excess. Prepare a brown hen hackle and catch it in by its bare stem just behind the eye.

5 Hold the hackle tip with a pair of hackle pliers and wind on three full turns. Secure the waste end of the hackle and remove.

6 Stroke the hackle fibers back along the body and fix in place with thread wraps. Catch in two white goose biots over the top of the body to form the wing. Trim off the excess before building a neat head. Cast off.

Scud

Brown trout

Cutthroat

Grayling

Rainbow trout

Scud, shrimp, call it what you will, this pattern imitates a small crustacean found in most rich lakes and rivers. Because of its curved, thickset shape, the Scud is a great pattern for packing full of lead, and by using wraps or layers of lead foil along the shank it can be tied very heavy. This allows it to be fished successfully in deep or fast-flowing water, where a lighter pattern simply wouldn't get down to the fish feeding on the bottom. Using a curved-shank shrimp hook, the Scud has a body of dubbed, blended fur over which a back of plastic raffia is stretched to provide a lifelike profile. To mimic the creature's legs, the fibers of fur under the hook are picked out with a dubbing needle.

Weight:
Adhesive lead foil

Rib:
Clear monofilament nylon

Shellback:
Olive plastic raffia

Thread:
Orange

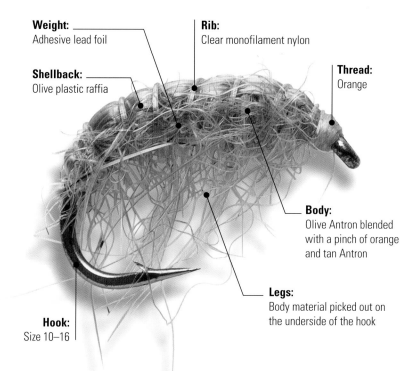

Body:
Olive Antron blended with a pinch of orange and tan Antron

Legs:
Body material picked out on the underside of the hook

Hook:
Size 10–16

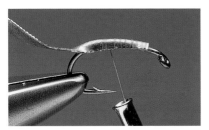

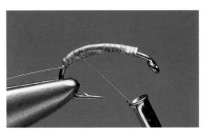

1 With the hook in the vise, fold a thin strip of adhesive lead foil over the shank. Using lead foil in this way will accentuate the humpbacked profile of the finished fly. Run the tying thread over the foil.

2 Cut away the excess foil and secure the end with tight thread wraps. Allow the foil to mold itself around the sides of the hook. At the end of the lead underbody, catch in 2 inches (5cm) of clear, monofilament nylon.

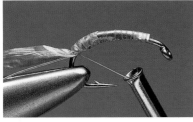

3 Take a short length of olive plastic raffia, a product sometimes known as Swiss Straw, and split it in two lengthways. Catch the raffia in at the same point as the nylon monofilament.

4 Blend together olive Antron with a small pinch each of orange and tan Antron. Dub the blend thickly onto the tying thread, and wind it over the lead foil and right up to the eye.

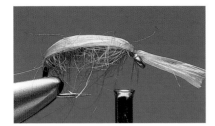

5 Wet the raffia slightly, which will help it to stretch, and pull it over the top of the body. Secure the loose end in place just behind the eye.

6 Wind the nylon monofilament in open, evenly spaced turns, up to the eye. Secure with tying thread and remove the excess monofilament and raffia. Cast off with a whip finish before teasing out the fur with a dubbing needle to form the legs.

133

Czech Nymph

Brown
trout

Grayling

Rainbow
trout

With the basic profile of a caseless caddis larva, the Czech Nymph is extremely effective when trout and grayling are feeding hard on the riverbed. Developed by Czech anglers, the combination of heavy hook and lead underbody ensures that the pattern sinks extremely quickly, making it ideal for fishing in deep or fast-moving water. The Czech Nymph may be tied in a range of colors, with brown and green being the most effective. The shellback consists of a thin, flexible plastic strip, a product marketed under brand names such as Body Stretch and Scud Back.

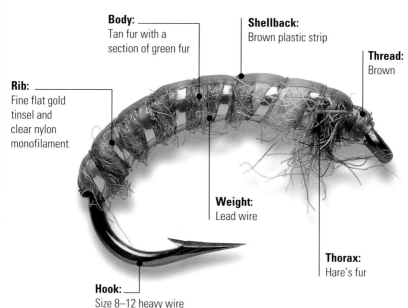

Body:
Tan fur with a
section of green fur

Shellback:
Brown plastic strip

Thread:
Brown

Rib:
Fine flat gold
tinsel and
clear nylon
monofilament

Weight:
Lead wire

Thorax:
Hare's fur

Hook:
Size 8–12 heavy wire

1 Fix the hook in the vise. Wind on close turns of medium-width lead wire to halfway around the bend, and secure with thread. At the rear of the underbody, catch in 3 inches (7.5cm) of clear nylon monofilament and a length of brown plastic strip.

2 Catch in 2 inches (5cm) of fine, flat, gold tinsel, then take a good pinch of tan fur and dub it thickly onto the tying thread. Wind the dubbed fur over the lead underbody, stopping halfway along.

3 Dub a small pinch of green fur onto the thread and wind it on to form a short, bright section in the body.

4 Dub on a good pinch of hare's fur and wind it up to the eye. Take hold of the flat, gold tinsel and wind it along the body in evenly spaced turns.

5 Secure the loose end of tinsel at the eye and remove it. Draw the plastic strip over the top of the body and secure it at the eye with tying thread.

6 Use the nylon monofilament as a rib, winding it over the body and the plastic shellback to lock it in place and suggest segmentation. Secure at the eye and remove the excess monofilament and plastic. Build a neat head before casting off.

135

Epoxy Buzzer

Brown trout

Rainbow trout

Flies that incorporate tough, epoxy resin are not limited just to saltwater patterns. The Epoxy Buzzer is tied to imitate a chironomid midge pupa. Most midge pupa imitations are tied in this around-the-bend style to mimic the curved body shape of the natural. The Epoxy Buzzer is designed to fish near the lake bottom, so, once tied, a coat of clear epoxy resin is applied. When tied on a heavyweight hook the result is a fly that not only sinks very quickly, but is also almost indestructible. When mixing the two-part epoxy resin, take care not to introduce any tiny bubbles that will reduce the clarity. Also, use a clear, quick-drying five-minute epoxy such as Devcon and only mix very small amounts at one time.

Body Finish:
Clear epoxy resin

Thorax Cover:
Pearl Lurex

Body:
Silver holographic tinsel

Rib:
Black tying thread

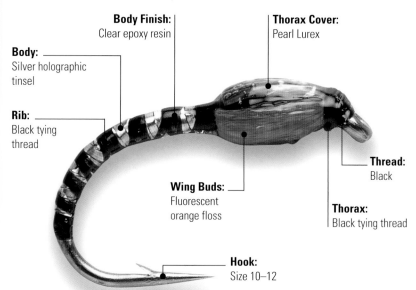

Thread:
Black

Wing Buds:
Fluorescent orange floss

Thorax:
Black tying thread

Hook:
Size 10–12

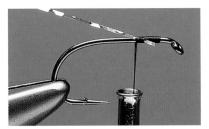

1 After fixing the hook in the vise, run the tying thread on at the eye. Wind on about ten turns, then catch in 4 inches (10cm) of silver holographic tinsel.

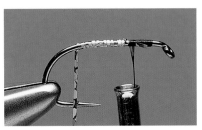

2 Wind the holographic tinsel over the bare shank, taking it well around the bend of the hook. Make sure that the turns are very close but do not overlap.

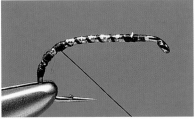

3 Wind the tying thread over the tinsel in open turns around the bend. Remove the excess tinsel. Now take the thread back along the shank by winding six close turns, then one open turn to produce a banded effect.

4 Once the tinsel's catching-in point has been reached, catch in four strands of fluorescent orange floss on both sides of the hook plus a short length of pearl Lurex on top.

5 Wind the tying thread repeatedly over the waste ends of the fluorescent floss to build up a pronounced thorax. Draw the floss strands forward and secure at the eye with tying thread.

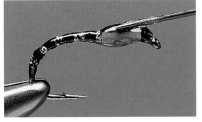

6 Draw the pearl Lurex over the back of the thorax and secure in the same position. Remove the excess Lurex and floss, build a small head, and cast off the tying thread. To finish, give the fly a coat of clear epoxy resin.

137

Ascending Midge Pupa

Brown
trout

Rainbow
trout

The pupae of the chironomid midge make up a large part of the
stillwater trout's diet, and the naturals are taken anywhere in the
water column, from the bottom to the surface. In order to rise to
the surface, where they will transpose into the adult, the pupae
buoy themselves up with gas. This gas forms a silvery sheen under
the pupae's skin, which in the Ascending Midge Pupa is imitated
by a thin strip of pearl Lurex tied along the top of the abdomen.
Unlike some midge pupa patterns, this is a close-copy imitation,
incorporating all of the major recognition points of the natural.
These include the white breathing filaments at the head and tail
plus the wing buds that are so noticeable in the real pupa.

Breathers:
White marabou

Wing Cases:
Gray feather fiber

Back:
Medium-width
pearl Lurex

Rib:
Clear nylon
monofilament

Thread:
Black

Body:
Black and red
feather fiber

Thorax:
Gray rabbit fur

Wing Buds:
Brown goose biots

Breathers:
White
marabou

Hook:
Size 12–16
caddis hook

1 Position the hook eye-down and secure it in the vise. Run the tying thread from the eye to well around the bend. Catch in three strands of white marabou and 1 inch (2.5cm) of medium-width pearl Lurex.

2 Catch in 2 inches (5cm) of clear nylon monofilament and two strands each of black and red feather fiber. Return the hook to the usual position. Keep the feathers next to each other and wind them around to cover two-thirds of the hook.

3 Secure the loose ends with thread and pull the pearl Lurex over the back of the body. Secure the Lurex in place by ribbing it with evenly spaced turns of the nylon monofilament.

4 Secure the monofilament with thread and remove all the waste ends. Take a slip of gray feather fiber and catch it in position in front of the body. Dub a small pinch of gray rabbit fur onto the thread and wind on one turn.

5 Trim the ends of two brown goose biots to a rounded shape and catch them in on both sides of the thorax to form wing buds. Take a few strands of white marabou and catch them in so that they project over the eye.

6 Dub on a larger pinch of rabbit fur and wind it from the wing buds to the eye. Pull the gray feather fiber over the thorax and divide the marabou in two. Secure it in place at the eye and cast off. Trim the marabou short at both ends.

Mudeye

Brown trout

Rainbow trout

Mudeye is the name Australians give to the nymph of the dragonfly, a large carnivorous insect that preys on smaller aquatic invertebrates. During the summer months, dragonfly nymphs break cover and crawl out onto dry land or along a reed stem before transposing into the winged adults. Trout will pick off the naturals as they leave the sanctuary of the lake bottom, so any imitation works best when fished around weed fringes or drowned timber. To add weight and help achieve the flattened body shape of the natural, a length of lead wire is secured on both sides of the hook shank before the dubbed body is applied. Threading green glass beads onto thick nylon monofilament forms the eyes. The ends of the nylon are then melted into a blob to hold the beads in place.

Body:
Dyed olive
rabbit fur

Wing Cases:
Olive cock pheasant tail

Thread:
Olive

Eyes:
Glass
beads

Thorax:
Dyed olive
rabbit fur

Hook:
Size 6–8 3X

Legs:
Knotted olive
feather fiber

Weight:
Thick lead wire

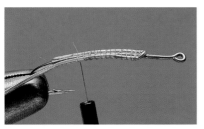

1 Fix the hook and run the tying thread to opposite the barb. Take 2 inches (5cm) of thick, lead wire and fold it so the bend is a little way short of the first thread wraps. Secure with thread so the ends lie along either side of the shank.

2 Remove the waste ends of lead at the bend. Applying the lead wire in this way creates a wide, weighted underbody. Cover the lead wire with thickly dubbed olive rabbit fur.

3 Take two slips of olive feather fiber, each containing three strands. Knot each slip once to suggest a joint and catch in on both sides of the body to form the rear legs.

4 Take another pinch of olive rabbit fur, dub it on, and wind on to form the first section of the thorax. Catch in two more legs, formed in the same way as the first pair, before adding another dubbed thorax section.

5 Wind the thread to the eye and catch in two glass beads attached to thick nylon monofilament. Catch in a slip of olive cock pheasant tail so that the butts project forward over the eye.

6 Remove the nylon ends and add the final thorax section. Pull the pheasant tail back between the eyes and secure with thread. Cast off. Reapply the thread behind the rear legs and fix the feather fibers. Cast off again and trim the fibers.

141

Marabou Damsel

Brown
trout

Rainbow
trout

Unlike the closely related dragonfly nymph, which propels itself by forcing water from its rear end, the nymph of the damselfly moves by a rapid lashing motion of its abdomen. This movement appears to act as a trigger to the fish, and for an imitation to be successful it needs to have plenty of built-in action. In the case of the Marabou Damsel, this is achieved by using a tuft of soft turkey marabou for the tail, a material that really pulses with life in the water. A plain dyed marabou may be used, but when a mottled feather is dyed olive the effect is very lifelike. In this pattern, marabou is also used for the slim body and legs. The eyes are formed from glass beads held in place on thick nylon monofilament, while the olive Ice Yarn thorax gives the pattern some extra sparkle.

Tail:
Olive mottled
marabou

Rib:
Fine gold wire

Body:
Olive mottled marabou

Wing Buds:
Olive feather
fiber

Eyes:
Glass beads

Thread:
Olive

Hook:
Size 10–12 3X

Legs:
Olive mottled
marabou

Thorax:
Olive Ice Yarn

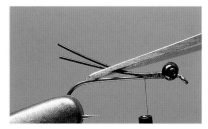

1 Fix the hook in the vise and run the tying thread on at the eye. Catch in two glass beads that have been attached to strands of thick nylon monofilament. Trim off the excess nylon.

2 Run the thread in touching turns down the shank and stop at a point opposite the hook barb. Catch in a pinch of olive mottled marabou as the tail.

3 At the base of the tail, catch in 3 inches (7.5cm) of fine, gold wire. At the same point, catch in a few strands of olive mottled marabou by their tips. Wind the marabou so that it covers two-thirds of the hook shank.

4 Secure the loose ends with tying thread and remove the waste. Rib the marabou body with evenly spaced turns of the gold wire and secure the waste end. Catch in a slip of olive feather fiber so that it projects over the eye.

5 Catch in a pinch of olive mottled marabou tips so that they, too, project over the eye. Dub on a pinch of olive Ice Yarn and wind it on as a thorax. The next step is to form the legs.

6 Divide the marabou into two bunches and fix them on both sides of the thorax by pulling the olive feather fiber first over the eyes and then over the back of the thorax. Secure with thread and trim the feather short to form wing buds. Cast off.

Rubber-legged Hare's Ear

The Hare's Ear Nymph already has a reputation as a deadly pattern when fishing either rivers or lakes. However, add some ultra-fine rubber legs and you have a pattern that twitches and pulses with life as it drifts with the current. Although standard rubber-legged patterns have been around for a long time, the introduction of very fine rubber strands has meant that the technique can be employed with virtually any type of nymph. These strands come in various diameters and in colors ranging from natural hues, such as brown and olive, to more garish yellows and purples.

Brown
trout

Cutthroat

Grayling

Rainbow
trout

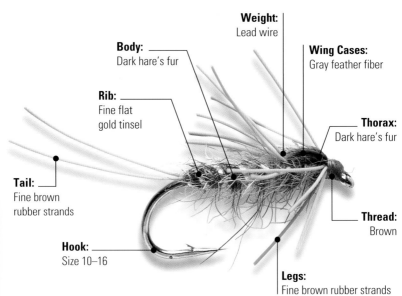

Weight:
Lead wire

Body:
Dark hare's fur

Wing Cases:
Gray feather fiber

Rib:
Fine flat
gold tinsel

Thorax:
Dark hare's fur

Tail:
Fine brown
rubber strands

Thread:
Brown

Hook:
Size 10–16

Legs:
Fine brown rubber strands

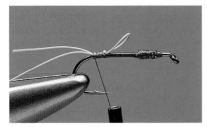

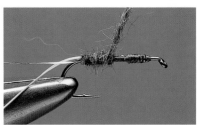

1 Fix the hook in the vise and wind on four turns of fine lead wire a little behind the eye. Trim the excess. Run on the tying thread just before the lead wire and wind it in close turns down to the bend. Catch in a doubled strand of fine rubber.

2 Catch in 2 inches (5cm) of fine, flat, gold tinsel at the tail base, then dub a pinch of dark hare's fur onto the thread. Wind the dubbed fur along the shank in close turns.

3 Stop winding the dubbed fur when it reaches the lead wire. Take hold of the gold tinsel and wind four open turns over the hare's fur.

4 Secure the loose end of tinsel and remove the excess. Take a fine, brown, rubber strand the length of the hook shank and catch it in halfway along its length.

5 Repeat the process on the other side of the body to create four legs. Catch in a slip of gray feather fiber before winding on a thorax of dubbed hare's fur.

6 Add further rubber strands at the eye—one or two on either side of the thorax will give plenty of movement. Pull the feather fiber over the back of the thorax and secure with tying thread.

Rubber-legged Stonefly Nymph

Brown trout

Cutthroat

Rainbow trout

This imitation of a giant black stonefly nymph is heavily weighted to allow it to be fished deep in pocket water and fast runs where the naturals are found. The weight comes from adhesive lead foil that is cut into a thin strip and wound over the hook shank prior to applying the body materials. The hook itself is a specially designed creeper model that has a slightly bent shank to give the finished fly a swimming attitude. The body and thorax, rather than simply black, are made from a blend of black Haretron to which small amounts of rust, orange, burgundy, and purple fur have been added to give a slightly mottled appearance. Although still effective without them, the addition of rubber legs gives the pattern the extra movement in the water that can make all the difference when presenting to selective trout.

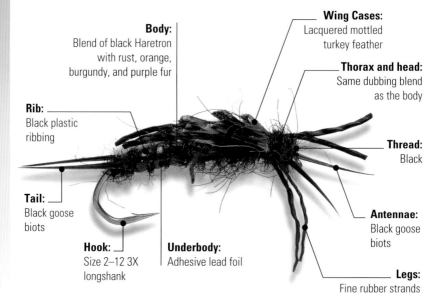

Body:
Blend of black Haretron with rust, orange, burgundy, and purple fur

Wing Cases:
Lacquered mottled turkey feather

Thorax and head:
Same dubbing blend as the body

Rib:
Black plastic ribbing

Thread:
Black

Tail:
Black goose biots

Antennae:
Black goose biots

Hook:
Size 2–12 3X longshank

Underbody:
Adhesive lead foil

Legs:
Fine rubber strands

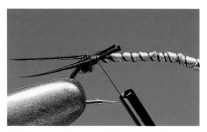

1 Wind on a strip of adhesive lead foil from the eye to the bend, creating a slight taper. Run the thread on at the eye and over the foil to the bend. Apply a small pinch of dubbing blend and wind it on to form a small ball behind the lead.

2 Take two black goose biots and catch one in on each side of the dubbing ball as the tail.

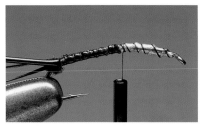

3 Catch in 3 inches (7.5cm) of black plastic ribbing so that the waste end covers half of the shank. Secure the waste end along the shank with thread to form an even base on which to apply the body.

4 Return the thread to the bend. Take a larger pinch of the fur blend and dub it thickly onto the tying thread. Wind it three-quarters of the way down the shank to form a chunky body. Wind the plastic ribbing over the body in close turns.

5 Secure the plastic and trim the excess. Spray the back of a mottled turkey feather with a flexible fixative and allow to dry. Remove a strip ¼-inch (6mm) wide. Cut a small V-shape from one end then catch it in place to form the wing cases.

6 Add a section of dubbed fur, then another strip of V-cut turkey feather. Repeat to form a third set of wing cases. Add two goose biots at the eye as antennae. Add two rubber strands on each side of the thorax and a head of dubbed fur. Cast off.

147

CHAPTER THREE

WET
FLIES

Wet flies have a very traditional background and were first developed on the lakes and rivers of western Europe. With such a long history, not surprisingly, most are tied with natural materials—furs and feathers that could be obtained from game birds, vermin, as a by-product of food production, or from the millinery trade.

Wet flies lend themselves to an impressionistic style of tying. Even those patterns that have been created to imitate a specific invertebrate mimic the colors and general form of the insect rather than looking like a close copy. Flies such as the Gosling best illustrate this point. In the right conditions it can actually be more effective than a close-copy imitation; however, it includes a hackle dyed bright orange, a color that is simply not found in the real mayfly. This trait is followed in many other wet flies, including the Blae and Black, which has a bright tail of golden pheasant tippet feather.

Wet flies can be subdivided into three separate groups. The simplest of all are the soft-hackle or spider patterns. These have just a body plus a few turns of hackle, and are very effective when fish are taking small mayfly nymphs or drowned insects. The next group, the palmers, have a hackle running the length of the body. This bushy style of tying lends itself to fishing in rough or broken water. The final group is the winged wet flies. These include wings tied to lie over the top of the body. They are often used to suggest a small mayfly, gnat, or other winged insect, but can be tied simply to arouse the fish's curiosity.

Diawl Bach

Brown
trout

Rainbow
trout

Of Welsh origin, the name means, literally, "Little Devil." Very quick and easy to tie, it is a great general-purpose nymph for lake fishing, where it can be used singly or as part of a team. There are now many variations on the Diawl Bach theme, some having dyed peacock herl bodies or ribs of colored holographic tinsel. This example, however, is where it all started, with the combination of a slim peacock herl body, ribbed with copper wire, and a few brown hackle fibers at the tail and throat. The key to success with this style of fly is to keep it quite sparse. It is normally tied on a heavy wired hook in sizes ranging from 10 to 14.

Body:
Peacock herl

Rib:
Fine copper wire

Tail:
Brown cock
hackle fibers

Thread:
Black or
brown

Hook:
Size 10–14

Hackle:
Brown cock
hackle fibers

150

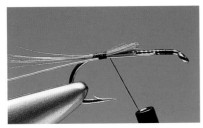

1 Fix the hook in the vise and run the tying thread down the shank to opposite the barb. At this point, catch in a few brown cock hackle fibers and 2 inches (5cm) of fine, copper wire, so that the waste ends lie along the shank.

2 Take two or three strands of peacock herl and catch them in by their tips at the same point as the tail and wire rib.

3 Wind the tying thread up to the eye in touching turns. This will form an even base for the body. Without twisting it, wind the peacock herl up to the eye. Secure the herl at the eye and remove the excess.

4 Hold the copper wire and wind it in evenly spaced turns, crossing the direction of the peacock herl. Secure the end and remove any excess.

5 Remove a few brown hackle fibers from the main feather. Check their length so that, when in place, the tips reach just past the hook point. Catch in under the eye.

6 Allow the hackle fibers to flare slightly under the hook to form a "false" or beard hackle. Complete with a small, neat head, casting off the thread with a whip finish.

151

Soft Hackle

Brown trout

Grayling

Rainbow trout

This deadly little fly looks like a cross between a nymph and a simple, hackled wet fly, and it is quick and easy to tie. The key to its success is the soft, highly mobile collar hackle. The feather used for this style of fly is normally a small game-bird feather such as gray partridge. The plumage of this bird has a subtle brown and tan mottling that makes it ideal for representing the legs of a small nymph or a drowned adult insect. When tying hackles from game-bird feathers, always tie the feather in by its tip, which is much finer than the thick base, and wind on only one or two turns of the feather to keep the effect very sparse. This example of the Soft Hackle has an orange body but other colors such as olive and black are also very effective.

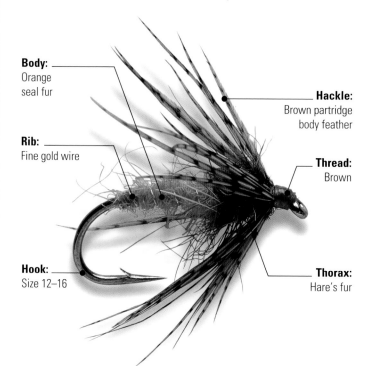

Body:
Orange
seal fur

Hackle:
Brown partridge
body feather

Rib:
Fine gold wire

Thread:
Brown

Hook:
Size 12–16

Thorax:
Hare's fur

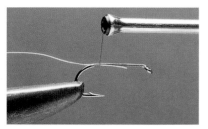

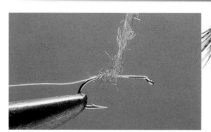

1 Having fixed the hook in the vise, run the tying thread down the shank, stopping at a point opposite the barb. Here, catch in 2 inches (5cm) of fine, gold wire.

2 Take a pinch of orange seal fur, or a manmade substitute, and dub it onto waxed tying thread with a simple finger-and-thumb twist. Wind the dubbed fur along the shank.

3 Having created a slim body with the orange fur, take hold of the gold wire and wind it over the body in open, evenly spaced turns. Secure the loose end of the wire with tying thread and remove the excess.

4 Dub on a small pinch of hare's fur and wind it on to form the thorax. Next, take a brown partridge body feather and stroke the fibers back and away from the tip. Catch the feather in at the eye by this exposed tip.

5 Take hold of the base of the partridge feather with hackle pliers. Wind on two or three turns of the feather, stroking the fibers back after each turn. Thick-stemmed feathers like these are always wound tip first.

6 Secure the loose end of the hackle with thread before removing the excess. Stroke the hackle fibers back along the body and fix in position with further turns of thread. Build a neat head and cast off.

153

Black Pennell

Brown
trout

Rainbow
trout

Atlantic
salmon

Sea trout

A traditional pattern, the Black Pennell is still widely used today on both rivers and lakes. In smaller sizes it works well during a hatch of black midge, while tied large, on a size 8 hook, it is a deadly pattern for sea trout and Atlantic salmon. Though some variations call for a dubbed fur body, the original Black Pennell has a body of floss silk. The aim is to create a very slim, sparse look, so bulk must be kept to a minimum. For this reason, when tying a floss body, the two-ply yarn is split and only one strand is used at a time.

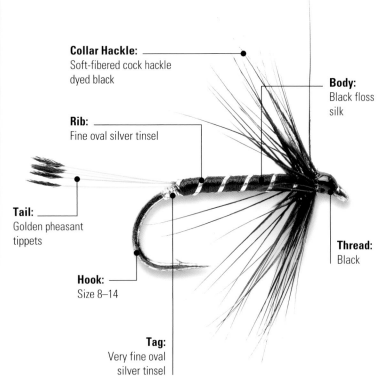

Collar Hackle:
Soft-fibered cock hackle
dyed black

Body:
Black floss
silk

Rib:
Fine oval silver tinsel

Tail:
Golden pheasant
tippets

Thread:
Black

Hook:
Size 8–14

Tag:
Very fine oval
silver tinsel

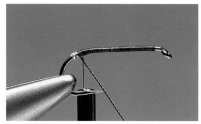

1 Fix the hook in the vise and run the tying thread down the shank to the bend. Catch in 2 inches (5cm) of very fine, oval, silver tinsel and wind on four turns as a tag. Secure the tinsel with thread and remove the waste end.

2 Take a few strands of golden pheasant tippet feather and catch them in to form the tail.

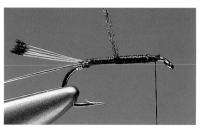

3 Allow the waste ends of the feather to lie along the shank. Catch in 2 inches (5cm) of oval, silver tinsel alongside the waste feather and cover the ends with thread.

4 Having formed a smooth base for the body, catch in 3 inches (7.5cm) of black floss silk at the eye. Allowing the floss to flatten, wind it to the tail, then back to the eye.

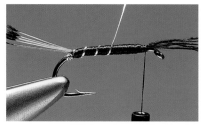

5 Secure the loose end of the floss at the eye. The double layer helps to create a smooth body. Wind on the fine, oval, silver tinsel in evenly spaced turns. Secure the tinsel with thread, then remove the excess tinsel and floss.

6 Prepare a dyed black cock hackle, leaving a short length of bare stem. Catch it in by the stem at the eye. Wind on two or three turns to create a sparse effect. Secure with thread and remove the excess before casting off.

Soldier Palmer

This bright red fly is a great favorite for loch-style fishing. With its bushy, palmered hackle, it works well on the top dropper of a three-fly cast. Palmering is a technique used for tying a hackle the entire length of the body. It is a method used for many traditional lake flies, where the density of hackling produces a fly that makes plenty of disturbance in the water's surface. It is also used on dry flies, particularly those that need to ride high in fast, broken water. The number of hackle turns may be varied to alter the overall density of the fly, with five turns the standard for a size 10 hook.

Brown trout

Rainbow trout

Sea trout

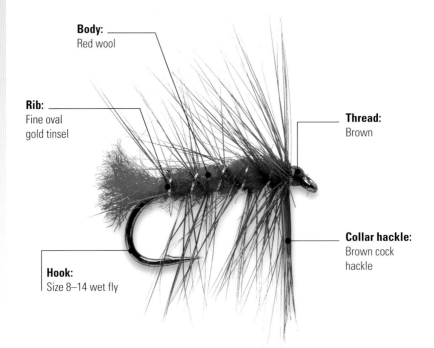

Body:
Red wool

Rib:
Fine oval
gold tinsel

Thread:
Brown

Collar hackle:
Brown cock
hackle

Hook:
Size 8–14 wet fly

1 Run the tying thread down the shank. Catch in a length of red wool so that the waste end lays the entire length of the shank. Cover the end with thread. At the tail base catch in 2 inches (5cm) of gold tinsel. Secure the waste end with thread.

2 Tease out a pinch of red wool and offer it up to the tying thread.

3 Dub the wool onto the thread to form a fluffy rope. Wind this in touching turns over the shank to form the body.

4 Prepare a brown cock hackle with fibers one-and-a-half times the hook gape, leaving a stub of bare stem. With the thread now just behind the eye, catch in the hackle. Use hackle pliers to wind the hackle right down to the tail, in open turns.

5 Wind the gold tinsel up through the hackle. Secure the tinsel at the eye and remove the excess.

6 With the hackle locked in place by the rib, remove the excess tip. Catch in a second hackle with longer fibers and wind as a collar. Build a neat head and cast off the thread.

157

Bibio

Brown
trout

Rainbow
trout

Atlantic
salmon

Sea trout

This is a great fly to use when fishing a gray, rolling wave. The
Bibio is of Irish origin, and was initially designed for catching sea
trout. It has, however, proved extremely successful for both
brown and rainbow trout when fishing large lakes and dams.
With a hackle running the length of the body (a technique
known as palmering), it is a bushy fly that, when pulled through
the water, creates a fish-attracting disturbance. The density of
this hackle can be altered depending on the number of turns
made. In this way, the Bibio can be tied effectively in either calm
or windy conditions. Effective sizes range from a size 8 down to
a size 14.

Body:
Black seal fur with a band
of red fur in the middle

Hackle:
Dyed black
cock hackle

Thread:
Black

Hook:
Size 8–14
wet fly

Rib:
Fine oval
silver tinsel

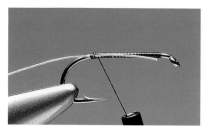

1 Once the hook is fixed in the vise, run the tying thread from the eye to a position opposite the barb. Catch in 2 inches (5cm) of fine, oval, silver tinsel, allowing the waste end to lie along the hook shank.

2 Secure the waste end to the hook with thread wraps. This will form an even base for the body. Dub on a pinch of black seal fur and wind it along one-third of the shank.

3 At this point, dub on an even smaller amount of red fur. Apply this to form a bright section.

4 Dub on another pinch of black seal fur the same size as the first. Wind it to the eye to form the third section of the body. Catch in a black cock hackle at the eye and, using a technique known as palmering, wind the hackle in evenly spaced turns along the length of the body.

5 Take hold of the fine, oval, silver tinsel and wind it so that it crosses each hackle turn.

6 At the eye, secure the tinsel and remove it, along with the excess hackle point. Catch in a second, longer-fibered hackle and wind on three turns to form a collar. Secure the waste end and trim before casting off.

159

Gosling

Brown
trout

Atlantic
salmon

The Gosling is a traditional Irish Lough pattern tied to represent
the large pale mayfly *Ephemera danica*. Unlike many mayfly
imitations it is tied, not as a dry fly, but to be used wet, pulled
through the wave tops. To create the bulk necessary to ensure
plenty of movement in the water, the Gosling has two hackles
at the collar. The first is a dyed orange cock hackle, over which
is wound a speckled gray mallard flank feather. The Gosling
is usually fished on either the point or top dropper of a
three-fly cast.

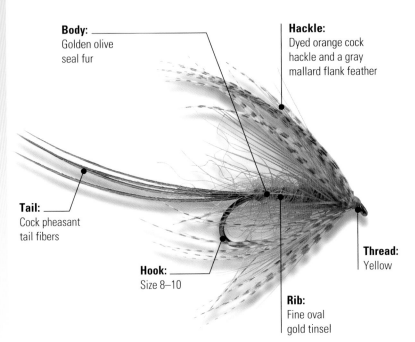

Body:
Golden olive
seal fur

Hackle:
Dyed orange cock
hackle and a gray
mallard flank feather

Tail:
Cock pheasant
tail fibers

Hook:
Size 8–10

Thread:
Yellow

Rib:
Fine oval
gold tinsel

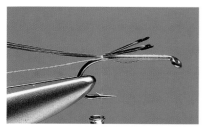

1 With the hook fixed in the vise, run the tying thread from the eye to the bend in touching turns. Catch in three fibers of cock pheasant tail and 2 inches (5cm) of fine, oval, gold tinsel.

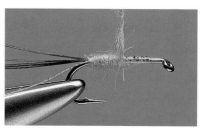

2 Take a pinch of golden olive seal fur and apply it to the tying thread. Dub it onto the thread to form a tapered rope. Wind the dubbed fur along the shank to just short of the eye.

3 Wind the gold tinsel over the dubbed body in evenly spaced turns.

4 Secure the end of the tinsel and remove the excess. Prepare a long-fibered, dyed orange cock hackle, leaving a short length of bare stem, and catch it in just behind the eye. Grasp the tip with hackle pliers and wind on three full turns.

5 Secure the loose hackle and trim the excess. Select a gray mallard flank feather and prepare it by stroking the fibers away from the tip. Catch the feather in by its tip just behind the eye.

6 Wind on the mallard feather, stroking the fibers back over the body after every turn. Two or three turns are sufficient. Secure the loose end and remove the excess. Cast off.

161

Brown
trout

Grayling

Rainbow
trout

Sea trout

Coachman

This simple, little wet fly has spawned a whole range of patterns that can be tied as either wet or dry flies. Most famous of all is the Royal Coachman, which, with an injection of red in its middle, is even tied as a bucktail. What all variations have in common is a body of peacock herl. This material, found in the eye train of the male peacock, has a wonderful iridescent effect. It can be wound as a single strand or used in multiples of two, three, or four, and twisted to form a thick, fluffy rope. Because peacock herl is not particularly tough, it can be protected by winding over wet varnish or by ribbing with wire or clear nylon monofilament.

Wing:
Slips of white duck wing quills

Body:
Peacock
herl

Thread:
Black

Hackle:
Brown cock hackle

Hook:
Size 8–16

1 Fix the hook in the vise and run the tying thread down the shank in touching turns. Stop opposite the hook barb and catch in three fibers of peacock herl.

2 Cover the waste ends with tying thread. Gently twist the fibers of peacock herl to form a fluffy rope. Wind this along the shank to form a plump body.

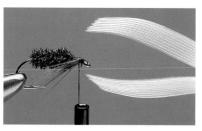

3 Secure the loose ends of herl with thread and remove the excess. Take a few fibers of brown cock hackle and catch them in as a beard hackle.

4 Select two slips from opposing white duck wing quills. Make sure that they are the same width and have similar curves. Place them together "curves in," to produce a straight wing.

5 Secure the wing on top of the eye with a winging loop. This technique prevents the wing from twisting around the hook.

6 When the wing is properly in position directly over the top of the body, fix it in place with tight thread wraps and remove the excess. Build a small, neat head and cast off.

163

Blae and Black

Brown
trout

Rainbow
trout

This traditional wet-fly pattern was designed to imitate the large
black midges that hatch from many lakes from spring to early
summer. Its Scottish roots are betrayed by the word "blae,"
which actually means blue and refers to the fly's blue-gray wing,
formed from starling or duck primary feather. Though a variation
of this pattern uses a dubbed body, the original uses floss silk.
To keep the effect smooth, the floss is wound in a double layer
starting a short distance from the eye. To prevent excess bulk
being created, fine rayon floss can be used or, when using
genuine silk floss, the two-ply strands are divided and only one
used at a time.

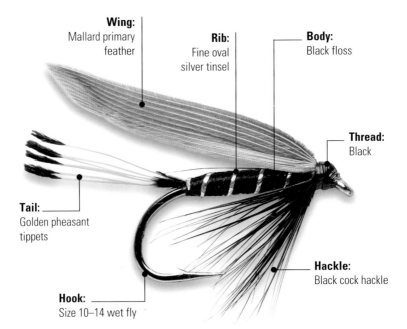

Wing:
Mallard primary
feather

Rib:
Fine oval
silver tinsel

Body:
Black floss

Thread:
Black

Tail:
Golden pheasant
tippets

Hackle:
Black cock hackle

Hook:
Size 10–14 wet fly

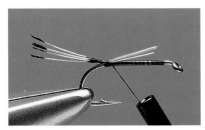

1 Having fixed the hook in the vise, run the tying thread down the shank in touching turns. Stop at a point opposite the barb and catch in a few strands of golden pheasant tippet.

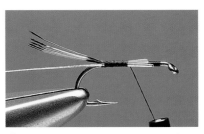

2 Secure the tippet strands with thread before catching in 2 inches (5cm) of fine, oval, silver tinsel at the base of the tail. Allow the waste ends to lie along the shank.

3 Wind the thread toward the eye, forming an even base for the body. A short distance from the eye, catch in 3 inches (7.5cm) of black floss. Wind the floss to the tail. Allowing the floss to spread flat will help create a smooth effect.

4 Wind the floss back up to the eye, secure the loose end with tying thread, then wind the tinsel over the body in evenly spaced turns. Secure the loose end of the tinsel with thread, and remove the excess tinsel and floss.

5 Catch in a black cock hackle at the eye and wind on three full turns.

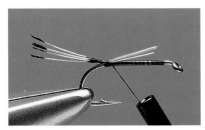

6 Stroke the fibers back and beneath the hook, and fix in place with thread wraps. Select a pair of mallard primary feather slips and catch in at the eye to form the wing. Cast off.

Silver Butcher

Brown trout

Rainbow trout

Sea trout

When this pattern was first tied it was known as the Moon Fly. Today, though, it has been renamed as part of a series of flies, most of which are based around a wing of iridescent blue mallard. All of the Butchers are flashy flies and used either as general attractants or, as in the case of the Silver Butcher, as a representation of a small fish. The technique for tying the wing is similar to most paired wet-fly wings. However, in the case of the Butcher, the material used is prone to splitting so it is very important to use a winging loop. Here each turn of thread made over the wing is always tightened with a direct downward pull. This prevents it from twisting around the body.

Wing:
Mallard blues

Rib:
Fine oval silver tinsel

Body:
Flat silver tinsel

Thread:
Black

Tail:
Red feather fiber

Hackle:
Black cock hackle

Hook:
Size 8–14 wet fly

166

1 Fix the hook in the vise and run the tying thread from the eye to opposite the barb. Catch in a slip of dyed red feather fiber and 2 inches (5cm) of fine, oval, silver tinsel.

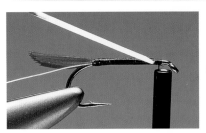

2 Allow the waste ends of feather and tinsel to lie along the shank and wind the tying thread up to the eye in touching turns to form an even base for the body. Take 4 inches (10cm) of flat, silver tinsel and catch it in at the eye.

3 Take hold of the flat tinsel and wind it down to the tail. Make sure each turn lies flat and that none overlap. Once the tail is reached, run the tinsel back to the eye in touching turns. Secure the tinsel with thread and remove the waste end.

4 With the double layer of flat tinsel in place, wind on the rib of fine, oval, silver tinsel in evenly spaced turns. Secure the end and remove any excess. Catch in a soft-fibered, dyed black cock hackle and wind on three turns.

5 Secure the hackle tip with thread and remove. Stroke the hackle fibers back and beneath the hook shank, and fix in place with tight thread turns.

6 Form a wing from two matched slips taken from opposite sides of a pair of mallard blues. Offer the slips up to the hook and secure with a winging loop. Cast off.

167

Teal, Blue, and Silver

Brown trout

Rainbow trout

Sea trout

Although a traditional wet fly, this pattern has all the hallmarks of a baitfish imitation, with its dark wing and sparkling, silver body. It is a great pattern for both lakes and rivers, and in its larger sizes works very well for night fishing for sea trout. When tying flat tinsel bodies, it is important to keep them smooth. To this end, the materials that are added first, such as the tail or rib, should be used to provide a flat, even base. A further trick is to use the tinsel in a double layer. Although real metal tinsel was originally used, today plastics such as Mylar are preferred because, although not quite as tough, they do not tarnish.

Wing:
Barred teal flank

Body:
Oval silver tinsel and flat silver Mylar

Tail:
Golden pheasant tippets

Thread:
Black

Throat hackle:
Cock hackle dyed blue

Hook:
Size 8–14 wet fly

168

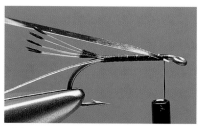

1 Wind the thread down the shank and catch in a tail of golden pheasant tippets and 2 inches (5cm) of silver tinsel. Return the thread to the eye and cover the waste ends. Cut the tip of a length of silver Mylar to a point and catch it in at the eye.

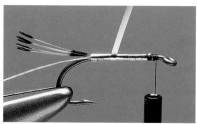

2 Wind the Mylar down to the tail in closely butted turns. Wind it back to its catching-in point, making sure that no turns overlap as this will ruin the smooth effect.

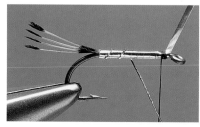

3 Secure the loose end of Mylar at the eye. Take hold of the oval, silver tinsel and wind it over the body in five evenly spaced turns. Secure the tinsel at the eye, and remove the excess tinsel and Mylar.

4 Prepare a bunch of blue cock hackles by removing any broken fibers from the bases, leaving short stubs of bare stem. Catch the hackles in on the underside of the hook. Trim off the excess butts of hackle fibers with scissors.

5 Select a slip of well-marked teal feather that is three times the width of the intended wing.

6 Fold one-third of the slip into the middle, then fold again to create a rolled wing slip. Catch this in on the top of the hook so the tip is level with that of the tail. Trim off the excess feather, build a neat head, and cast off the tying thread.

March Brown

Brown trout

Rainbow trout

Originally tied as an imitation of a specific species of mayfly, the March Brown has since been used as a more general and highly effective wet fly. The key to its success is the combination of hare's fur, partridge hackles, and hen pheasant wing to produce a very natural effect that works well on trout feeding on nothing in particular. When using hare's fur for a body, it is important to use both the softer underfur and the stiffer, spiky guard hairs to add a bit of life. The softer fur acts as a "carrier" for the guard hairs, and blending the two together makes the dubbing process easier.

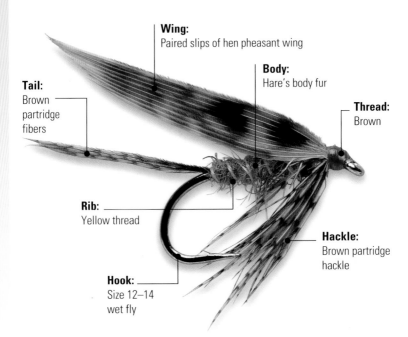

Wing:
Paired slips of hen pheasant wing

Body:
Hare's body fur

Tail:
Brown partridge fibers

Thread:
Brown

Rib:
Yellow thread

Hackle:
Brown partridge hackle

Hook:
Size 12–14 wet fly

1 Once the hook is fixed in the vise, run the tying thread down the shank to a point opposite the barb. Catch in a tail of brown partridge fibers and 2 inches (5cm) of yellow thread.

2 Take a pinch of hare's fur containing a small amount of the stiffer guard hairs. Dub it onto the tying thread to form a thin, tapered rope. Wind the dubbed hare's fur along the shank, stopping a short distance from the eye.

3 Take hold of the yellow thread and wind it over the body in open turns.

4 Secure the loose end of the thread rib at the eye and remove the excess. Take a short-fibered partridge hackle and stroke the fibers back from the tip.

5 Cut the tip short with scissors and use it to catch the hackle in at the eye. Take hold of the hackle with hackle pliers and wind on three full turns.

6 Stroke the fibers back and fix in position with thread wraps. Remove any excess. Place together matched slips of hen pheasant wing quill and catch in as a wing. Cast off the tying thread.

Invicta

Brown trout

Rainbow trout

Sea trout

Although very traditional in form, having been designed in the late nineteenth century by British angler James Ogden, the Invicta is still widely used today. It is a complex pattern and involves tricky procedures such as palmering, where the hackle is wound the length of the body, adding a blue jay throat hackle, and rolling a slip of hen pheasant center tail feather. However, once all the techniques used to tie the Invicta have been mastered, most other patterns can be tackled with confidence. This yellow-bodied version is the original, but the pattern now has many other popular variations including the Silver Invicta, the Green Invicta, and the White Hackled Invicta to name but a few.

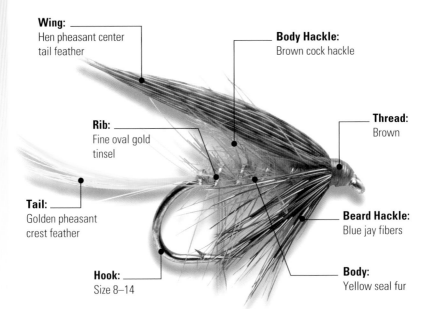

Wing: Hen pheasant center tail feather

Body Hackle: Brown cock hackle

Rib: Fine oval gold tinsel

Thread: Brown

Tail: Golden pheasant crest feather

Beard Hackle: Blue jay fibers

Hook: Size 8–14

Body: Yellow seal fur

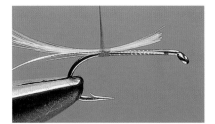 

1 Secure the hook in the vise. Run on the tying thread, stopping opposite the barb of the hook. At this point, catch in 2 inches (5cm) of fine, oval, gold tinsel plus a tail of golden pheasant crest feather.

2 Apply a pinch of yellow seal fur or substitute to the tying thread. Dub the fur onto the thread and wind the resulting rope over the hook shank, stopping a little short of the eye.

3 Select a brown cock hackle with fibers slightly longer than the gape of the hook. Catch the hackle in place at the eye by its base and grasp the tip with hackle pliers. Wind it over the fur body in open, evenly spaced turns.

4 Once the hackle has reached the end of the body, begin winding the gold tinsel up through the hackle in evenly spaced turns. To retain tension, keep the hackle pliers in place until the first few hackle turns are locked in by the tinsel.

5 Remove any excess hackle tip plus the waste end of the tinsel. Next, tear off a bunch of blue jay fibers and catch them in beneath the hook to form a beard hackle.

6 Take a slip of hen pheasant center tail feather that is three times the width of the intended wing. Fold one edge of the slip to its center, then fold the slip in half and catch in the prepared feather at the eye. Create a neat head and cast off.

Curry's Red Shrimp

Atlantic salmon

Curry's Red Shrimp is acknowledged as the pattern from which all other Irish-style shrimp flies evolved. It is used exclusively for catching Atlantic salmon, works well in a variety of water conditions, and is especially good in small- to medium-sized spate rivers. Although extremely impressionistic as far as imitating a real shrimp is concerned, the pattern employs a mixture of feathers to add plenty of movement. Of most interest is the tail, which imitates the shrimp's whiskers and consists of a golden pheasant breast feather wound on at the bend. This tail should always be tied long, but can vary between quite full to sparse, depending on the type of water in which it is to be used.

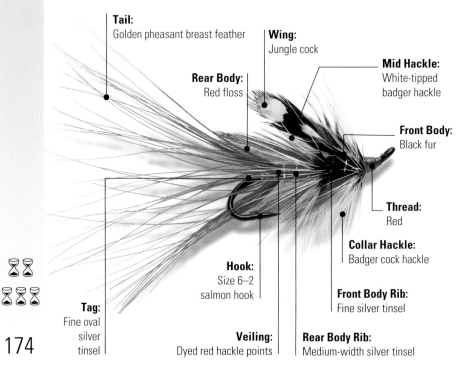

Tail:
Golden pheasant breast feather

Wing:
Jungle cock

Mid Hackle:
White-tipped badger hackle

Rear Body:
Red floss

Front Body:
Black fur

Thread:
Red

Collar Hackle:
Badger cock hackle

Hook:
Size 6–2 salmon hook

Front Body Rib:
Fine silver tinsel

Tag:
Fine oval silver tinsel

Veiling:
Dyed red hackle points

Rear Body Rib:
Medium-width silver tinsel

1 Run on the thread and catch in 2 inches (5cm) of fine, oval, silver tinsel. Run the thread a short way up the shank, then wind on four turns of tinsel. Select a golden pheasant breast feather, trim the tip short and catch it in just in front of the tag.

2 Grasp the base of the feather with hackle pliers and wind on three turns. As each turn is made, stroke the fibers back past the hook bend. Secure the fibers in position and remove the waste.

3 Catch in 3 inches (7.5cm) of medium-width silver tinsel, then wind the thread halfway back to the eye. Catch in a length of red floss and wind it back to the tail to form the rear body. Secure the loose end and remove the excess.

4 Wind the tinsel rib over the body in evenly spaced turns. Secure with thread and remove any excess. Catch in two pairs of dyed red hackle points above and below the body to act as veiling.

5 Apply a white tipped badger hackle at the mid-section. Dub on a black fur front body section and rib it with fine, silver tinsel. Add another set of red hackle point veils and a wing of jungle cock.

6 Trim all the waste ends. Complete with a collar of badger cock hackle, and cast off.

CHAPTER FOUR

STREAMERS

Streamers are tied to be very mobile, using soft feathers to give them plenty of action. Streamers can fulfill a variety of roles, from the imitative, where they are used to mimic the color and shape of small baitfish, to the more impressionistic, with gaudy patterns designed to trigger the fish's aggression or curiosity.

While feathers are not as robust a winging material as hair, they do have the advantage of imparting a great deal of mobility and life to the fly. Various types of feathers are used, though in many older patterns cock neck or saddle hackles are used for the wing. These are tied in as opposing pairs so that the curves of the feathers cancel one another out and produce a perfectly straight  wing. Hackle feather wings are normally tied in at the eye so that they lie low over the body and project well past the hook bend.

While cock hackles are still used, the material now takes second place to turkey marabou as the most commonly used feather for winging streamers. Being soft and highly mobile, marabou produces an absolutely wonderful action in the water. It is also a great deal easier to apply than cock hackles. Because of its superb action, marabou is also widely used as a tail. In patterns such as the Woolly Bugger and Tadpole, a long, mobile  tail produces an allure that game fish of all kinds find difficult to resist. Marabou works well in all water types but lends itself particularly well when fishing in stillwater where there is no current to give the fly movement and all the action must be imparted by the retrieve.

Black Ghost

This is a very traditional style of streamer, but still very effective on both lakes and rivers. It uses paired cock hackles for the wing, placed back-to-back and tied in at the head. When using hackles in this way, it is important that they are of similar size. Check that the fibers are undamaged and then place the pairs of hackles together, dull-sides in. Hackles have a natural curve to them, and putting them together so that they curve toward one another means that they cancel each other out and produce a straight wing. Two pairs of feathers are enough to produce the correct wing density.

Brown trout

Arctic char

Cutthroat

Rainbow trout

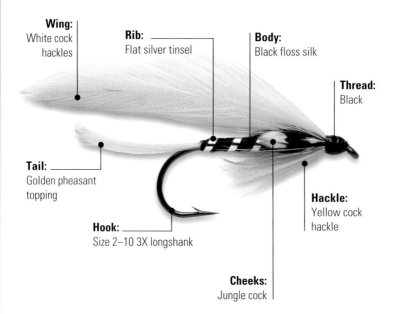

Wing:
White cock hackles

Rib:
Flat silver tinsel

Body:
Black floss silk

Thread:
Black

Tail:
Golden pheasant topping

Hook:
Size 2–10 3X longshank

Hackle:
Yellow cock hackle

Cheeks:
Jungle cock

1 Fix the hook in the vise and, opposite the barb, catch in a golden pheasant topping and 3 inches (7.5cm) of flat, silver tinsel. From the eye, wind on a body of black floss silk and rib it with the tinsel. Secure the tinsel and remove the excess.

2 Tear off a bunch of dyed yellow cock hackle fibers and catch them in as a beard hackle.

3 Take two pairs of white cock hackles from opposite sides of the cape. Place them together, dull-sides in, so that the natural curves cancel one another out.

4 Judge the wing for length so that it projects just past the tail, then tear off all the fibers further down the hackle stalks. Catch in the wing with tight thread wraps.

5 Use further turns of thread to position the wing low over the body. Then, instead of trimming them off, fold the stalks over and secure with more thread wraps.

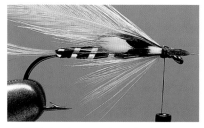

6 With the wing secured, add cheeks of jungle cock to either side. Complete by forming a neat, tapered head, and cast off the thread with a whip finish.

Olive Matuka

Brown trout

Cutthroat

Rainbow trout

The term Matuka originally applied to a specific New Zealand bird whose feathers were used for this style of fly. The term has since come to mean a winging style where the feathers are secured to the top of the body with turns of ribbing. The great advantage of this method is that it prevents the wing from twisting or getting caught under the bend of the hook while casting. The wing is prepared in the standard way of forming a streamer wing, using pairs of cock hackles placed back to back. Only then are the fibers torn away from the underside of the wing so that it can sit easily on the body.

Wing/Tail:
Dyed olive grizzle cock hackles

Rib:
Oval gold tinsel

Thread:
Olive

Hook:
Size 2–10 3X longshank

Body:
Dyed olive rabbit fur

Hackle:
Dyed olive grizzle hackles

Weight:
Lead wire

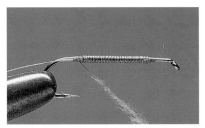

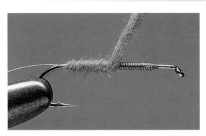

1 Fix the hook in the vise and form a lead wire underbody. Run on the tying thread and catch in 3 inches (7.5cm) of oval, gold tinsel at the bend. Dub on a generous pinch of dyed olive rabbit fur.

2 Using a simple twisting action between finger and thumb, work the rabbit fur into a tapering rope. Wind the rope in touching turns along the hook shank.

3 Select two pairs of grizzle cock hackles dyed olive. Place them dull-sides together so that all the tips are level. This will form a straight wing.

4 Remove the fibers at the base so the wing is the correct length. Then, tear off the fibers under the wing for the same length as the body. Catch in at the eye.

5 Moisten the wing and pull it over the body. Divide the hackle fibers at the tail and make one turn with the tinsel. Wind the tinsel through the hackles in evenly spaced turns, dividing the hair as you go.

6 Add a collar of dyed olive grizzle hackle and cast off.

Alaskabou

Coho
salmon

Steelhead

Chinook
salmon

The Alaskabou pattern is quick and easy to tie, and packed with fish-catching action. This is the purple version of a range of similarly tied patterns that are particularly effective for steelhead and the various species of Pacific salmon. The key to the pattern's action is a dense wing of dyed turkey marabou that pulses with life as it swings around in the current. The hackle, too, has plenty of mobility because it is tied from a Schlappen feather—a hackle taken from below the saddle patch of a cockerel. This particular feather has the same shape and tying properties as a standard cock saddle hackle, but with much softer fibers. Other effective colors in the Alaskabou range include pink, orange, and chartreuse. This pattern is so quick to tie because there is no body, just a wing and hackle.

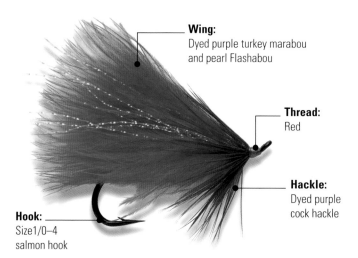

Wing:
Dyed purple turkey marabou
and pearl Flashabou

Thread:
Red

Hackle:
Dyed purple
cock hackle

Hook:
Size1/0–4
salmon hook

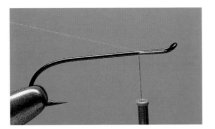

1 After fixing the hook in the vise, run the tying thread on at the eye. When using loop-eyed salmon hooks, tight thread wraps should be wound over the loop to prevent any chance of it opening when a fish is hooked.

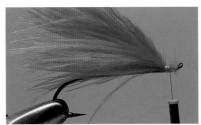

2 Take a large bunch of dyed purple turkey marabou and catch it in at the eye using tight thread wraps, so that the tips of the wing project just past the hook bend.

3 Take a few strands of pearl Flashabou or Crystal Hair and catch them in place on both sides of the wing. These tinsel strands give the wing a real sparkle.

4 Trim the excess tinsel over the eye. Select a dyed purple cock hackle with soft fibers that is approximately twice the length of the hook gape. Prepare it, leaving a short length of bare stem, and catch in the stem at the eye.

5 Take hold of the hackle tip with a pair of hackle pliers and wind on three or four full turns to form a dense collar.

6 Secure the loose hackle tip with thread and remove. Stroke the hackle fibers back so that they sweep over the wing then fix them in position with turns of tying thread. Build a small, neat head with the thread, then cast off with a whip finish.

183

Viva

Brown
trout

Rainbow
trout

Black and green is a great color combination for early season
stillwater patterns. The Viva, named after a 1960s British car
model, is a lure that combines just these colors, with a black
wing and body contrasted by a fluorescent lime-green tail. To
provide a dense silhouette, the body is made of chenille and
capped with a generous wing of dyed black turkey marabou.
The marabou not only creates the right profile, but being soft
and highly mobile, it gives the pattern plenty of action. When
using marabou as a wing, the fiber tips should be kept level with
one another. If any need trimming, this is best done by pinching
them off with a thumbnail, rather than using scissors that
produce a straight, unnatural finish.

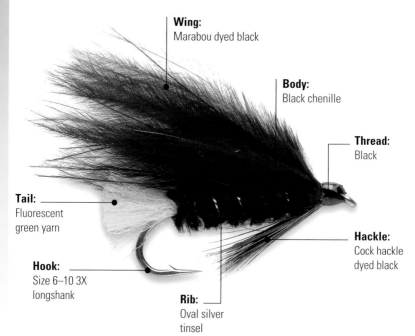

Wing:
Marabou dyed black

Body:
Black chenille

Thread:
Black

Tail:
Fluorescent
green yarn

Hook:
Size 6–10 3X
longshank

Rib:
Oval silver
tinsel

Hackle:
Cock hackle
dyed black

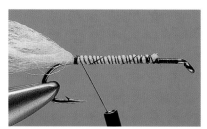

1 Secure the hook in the vise and run the tying thread to a point opposite the barb. Fold double a strand of fluorescent green yarn and catch in place. Lie the waste ends along the shank and cover with tying thread.

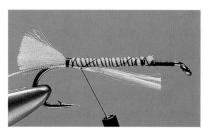

2 Trim the yarn short to form the tail. Take 3 inches (7.5cm) of oval, silver tinsel and tease out one end to reduce the bulk. Catch the tinsel in at the base of the tail, with the teased end under the shank.

3 Take 4 inches (10cm) of black chenille and expose a short length of the core from one end. Catch the chenille in by the core at the base of the tail.

4 Wind the tying thread up to the eye, taking in the frayed tinsel. Using fingers or hackle pliers, grip the chenille and wind it in touching turns along the shank to the thread.

5 Secure the loose end of the chenille and remove it with scissors. Wind the oval, silver tinsel over the chenille in evenly spaced turns. Secure and remove the waste end of the tinsel.

6 Apply a beard hackle of black cock hackle fibers. Add a wing of black marabou so the tips fall just past the tail. Cast off.

185

Appetizer

Brown trout

Rainbow trout

This pattern was developed by Bob Church specifically to imitate the small baitfish found in many lakes and reservoirs. It was one of the first British patterns to incorporate marabou, which Church used to give the pattern the movement of a small fish. The Appetizer also has an overwing of gray squirrel tail, which, although "dumbing down" the action of the marabou, gives some control and also suggests the darker back of the fish. The tail and hackle are both a blend of gray mallard flank feather and orange and green hackle fibers. When tying a beard, or "false" hackle, the fibers should flare evenly under the hook. Inverting the hook in the vise can make this process easier.

Body:
White chenille

Rib:
Fine oval
silver tinsel

Tail:
Orange and green
hackle fibers mixed
with speckled gray
mallard

Wing:
White marabou with a pinch
of gray squirrel over the top

Hook:
Size 6–8 3X
longshank or two
in tandem

Hackle:
Orange and green
hackle fibers mixed
with speckled gray
mallard

1 Secure the hook in the vise and run the tying thread from the eye to the bend. Take a few fibers each of gray mallard and orange and green cock hackle fibers, and catch them in as a tail.

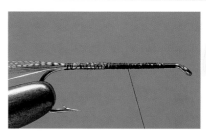

2 At the same point catch in 3 inches (7.5cm) of fine, oval, silver tinsel. Leave the waste end long, doubling it back to form an even base for the body. Cover the waste ends with thread.

3 Cut 4 inches (10cm) of white chenille. Expose a short section of the core and catch it in at the tail. Wind in touching turns to the eye. Wind even turns of the silver tinsel over the chenille to form the rib. Secure and remove the excess.

4 Take the same colors of hackle fibers as used for the tail and catch them in at the eye. If necessary, invert the hook in the vise to make applying the hackle easier.

5 Return the hook to its original position. Select a generous pinch of white marabou and catch it in as the wing. The tips should be level with those of the tail.

6 Remove a bunch of gray squirrel tail fibers and position them over the marabou. The tips of the hair should reach the end of the body. Fix in place and trim the waste ends. Wind a neat head and cast off with a whip finish.

187

Black Tadpole

Brown
trout

Rainbow
trout

In rivers, the current imparts movement to the fly; on lakes, all that action must come from the retrieve and the fly itself. Turkey marabou, which is extremely soft, has been used for many years to make highly mobile wings and tails for stillwater work. In the Tadpole, this feature is taken to its logical conclusion, with a highly mobile tail that is much longer than its body. By adding weight to the hook, the Tadpole is made to duck and dive on every twitch of the retrieve, while the long tail pulses with life. It is an action few trout are able to resist. Tadpoles are tied in a variety of colors, from olive, orange, and white to this black and green combination.

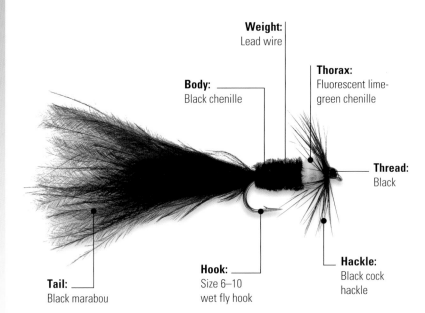

Weight:
Lead wire

Thorax:
Fluorescent lime-
green chenille

Body:
Black chenille

Thread:
Black

Hackle:
Black cock
hackle

Tail:
Black marabou

Hook:
Size 6–10
wet fly hook

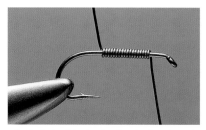

1 Fix the hook in the vise. Starting just short of the eye, wind on touching turns of lead wire to form a weighted underbody. Stop opposite the hook point to leave a small gap to the bend.

2 Run on the tying thread at the eye and wind it in close turns over the lead wire. Catch in a long bunch of black marabou at the bend.

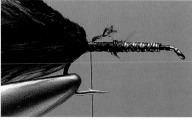

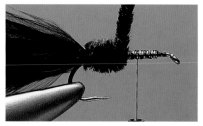

3 Take 3 inches (7.5cm) of black chenille and expose the core at one end. Catch it in at the base of the tail using the bare section. Securing the tail and chenille in the gap to the rear of the underbody stops an unsightly bump from forming.

4 Wind the chenille around the hook in close turns until it covers two-thirds of the shank. Trim the chenille, secure the waste end, and remove the excess.

5 Catch in a length of lime-green chenille and wind it to a point just short of the eye. Secure the end of the chenille with thread and remove the excess.

6 Catch in a black cock hackle and wind on three turns. Stroke the fibers back and secure with thread before casting off.

Woolly Bugger

This is a very versatile pattern that will catch fish on virtually any lake or river. The key to its success is plenty of action, provided by a closely palmered hackle and a tail of soft turkey marabou. It also has a heavily weighted underbody formed from close turns of lead wire. These are applied before the thread and can either be held in place with strong glue or by tight thread wraps. The Woolly Bugger is tied in a variety of color combinations, usually natural ones such as black, brown, and olive, and can imitate anything from a leech or dragonfly nymph to a small fish. The black and olive version is particularly effective. The hook needs to be removed from the vise to allow the glue to dry, so it is worth making up a batch of underbodies at the same time.

Brown trout

Arctic char

Cutthroat

Rainbow trout

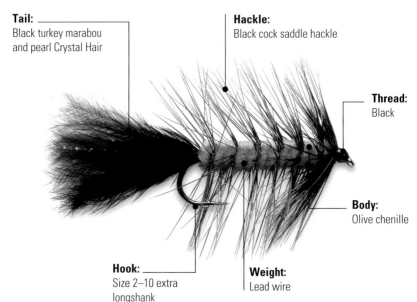

Tail:
Black turkey marabou and pearl Crystal Hair

Hackle:
Black cock saddle hackle

Thread:
Black

Body:
Olive chenille

Hook:
Size 2–10 extra longshank

Weight:
Lead wire

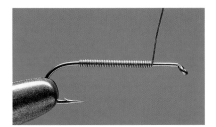

1 Secure the hook in the vise. Starting just after the bend, wind on close turns of lead wire to form the weighted underbody. Apply a coat of strong glue, then remove the hook from the vise and leave to dry, securing the hook upright in a piece of foam.

2 Replace the hook in the vise. Run the tying thread on at the eye and carry it down to the bend, past the end of the lead. Catch in a short bunch of black turkey marabou.

3 Secure the marabou with tight thread wraps, allowing the waste ends to fill the gap left at the rear of the lead wire. Take a strand of pearl Crystal Hair twice the length of the tail. Fold it in half and catch in at the tail base.

4 Prepare a black saddle hackle by stroking the fibers back from the tip, then catch it in at the base of the tail. Take 3 inches (7.5cm) of olive chenille and remove a section to leave a bare core. Use this core to catch the chenille in at the tail base.

5 Take the tying thread to the eye and wind the chenille on in touching turns to a point just short of the eye.

6 Secure the loose end of the chenille with tying thread and remove the excess. Wind the hackle up to the eye in evenly spaced turns. At the eye, make three close turns to form a collar. Secure and remove the excess. Cast off the thread.

191

Babine Special

Coho
salmon

Steelhead

Chinook
salmon

Arctic
char

Grayling

The Babine Special is a deadly pattern for a whole range of species from trout and steelhead to salmon, char, and grayling. It is at its best when the target species is feeding on salmon eggs, which the pattern is designed to imitate. The body comprises two egg-shaped sections that are tied from either fluorescent chenille or Glo-bug yarn, the latter being spun and clipped into an egg shape. When using chenille for this style of fly, choose one with a large diameter, and overlap the turns rather than winding them side by side, to help create the desired shape.

Body:
Two balls of
fluorescent
orange chenille
or Glo-bug yarn

Thread:
Red

Tail:
Short tuft of
white marabou

Hook:
Size 2–6 single
salmon hook

Hackle:
White cock hackle
in front of both
sections

1 Fix the hook in the vise, wind the thread in close turns over the loop eye, and carry it to the bend. Catch in a bunch of white marabou and pinch it short rather than cutting it. Allow the waste ends to lie along the shank and cover with thread turns.

2 Take 3 inches (7.5cm) of chenille, expose the core at one end, and catch in.

3 Wind the tying thread halfway back along the hook shank. Take hold of the chenille, with either the fingers or hackle pliers, and begin to wind.

4 To create the required egg shape, wind the turns of chenille next to one another but allowing them to overlap in the center of the egg shape. Finish it at the point where the chenille meets the tying thread.

5 Secure the loose end of the chenille and remove the excess. Prepare a white cock hackle, leaving a short stub of bare stem, and catch it in at the front of the body. Using hackle pliers, wind on three turns. Secure and remove the excess.

6 Add a second chenille egg in exactly the same way as the first. Prepare a second hackle with slightly longer fibers than the first. Wind on three turns at the eye, then secure the tip and remove any excess. Cast off the thread.

Marabou Muddler

Brown trout

Arctic char

Cutthroat

Rainbow trout

While this yellow and gold version of the Marabou Muddler works extremely well, the pattern can also be tied in a wide range of colors. In white and silver it makes a great imitation of a silvery bait fish, while in olive or brown it can be used to suggest anything from a leech to a small bottom-dwelling fish. In all its variations, the basic techniques and materials remain the same. Its pulsating, fish-attracting action comes from a generous wing of turkey marabou while the bulky deer hair head makes plenty of subsurface disturbance on the retrieve. The pattern can be fished at all depths, but on those variations designed to work close to the lake or riverbed, a weighted underbody is used.

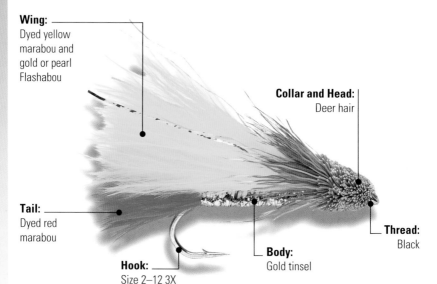

Wing:
Dyed yellow marabou and gold or pearl Flashabou

Collar and Head:
Deer hair

Tail:
Dyed red marabou

Thread:
Black

Hook:
Size 2–12 3X

Body:
Gold tinsel

194

1 Secure the hook in the vise and run the tying thread down the shank to the bend. There, catch in a tuft of dyed red marabou for the tail. Allow the waste ends of the marabou to lie along the hook shank.

2 Wind open turns of thread over the waste ends of marabou to form an even base for the body. Catch in 4 inches (10cm) of gold tinsel at the base of the tail, again using the waste end to create an even base over which to wind the body.

3 Take hold of the gold tinsel and begin to wind it along the shank. Make sure that each turn overlaps slightly—this helps to create an even effect. Carry the tinsel toward the eye until it covers three-quarters of the hook shank.

4 Secure the loose end of the tinsel and remove the excess. Next, take a generous plume of dyed yellow marabou and catch it in place just in front of the body with tight thread turns. Make sure that the wing tip is level with that of the tail.

5 Add a few fibers of gold or pearl Flashabou over the top of the wing. Then offer a bunch of deer hair up to the hook so that the tips project back over the wing. Wind three turns of thread over the hair pulling it tight so that the hair flares.

6 As the deer hair flares and spins around the hook, the tips will form the collar. Secure the hair with tight thread wraps, adding further bunches until the gap up to the eye is filled. Cast off the thread and trim the hair to a neat bullet shape.

Muddler Minnow

Brown
trout

Arctic
char

Cutthroat

Rainbow
trout

Steelhead

This is the original Don Gapen pattern that spawned, literally, thousands of flies that now carry the Muddler appellation. First designed to imitate a small bottom-dwelling fish, Muddlers are now tied as general attractor patterns and to imitate anything from caddis flies to grasshoppers. While each Muddler may differ in color and profile, all have the same basis in their construction: the spinning and clipping of deer hair to create a buoyant head or body. Being hollow and easily compressed, deer hair can be flared on the hook to form a ruff. By adding more bunches and compacting them, the hair is made dense enough to be shaped by trimming with scissors or a blade. When tying Muddlers it pays to use a strong thread that allows plenty of pressure to be applied to the hair.

Wing:
Gray squirrel hair
and mottled turkey
feather

Body:
Flat gold
Mylar tinsel

Rib:
Medium-width
oval gold tinsel

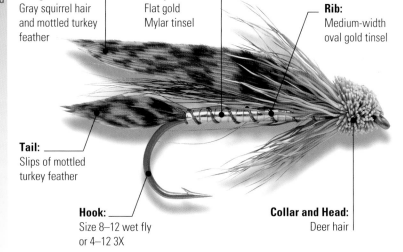

Tail:
Slips of mottled
turkey feather

Hook:
Size 8–12 wet fly
or 4–12 3X

Collar and Head:
Deer hair

196

1 After fixing the hook in the vise, run the tying thread from the eye to a point opposite the barb. Take two opposing slips of mottled turkey feather, place them together so the tips are level, and catch them in as the tail.

2 Catch in 3 inches (7.5cm) of medium-width, oval, gold tinsel, winding the thread, in close turns, three-quarters of the way back to the eye. Catch in 4 inches (10cm) of flat, gold, Mylar tinsel and wind it in touching turns back to the tail.

3 Wind the Mylar back to its catching-in point and secure. Rib the body with even turns of the gold tinsel. Secure and remove the excess of both tinsels. Catch in a slim wing of gray squirrel tail so that the tips are level with those of the tail.

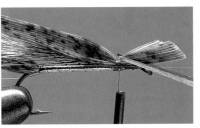

4 Select two more opposing slips of mottled turkey wing and place them together, dull sides out. Secure the slips in place over the top of the hair wing, again so that all the tips are level. Trim the waste ends.

5 Cut a good bunch of deer hair from the skin. Place the hair on top of the hook so that the tips lie back along the wing. Wind on two or three loose turns of tying thread.

6 Pull the thread tight. This will cause the hair to flare around the hook, producing a collar and the base of the Muddler head. Add further bunches of deer hair in this way until the eye is reached. Cast off the thread and trim the head to shape.

Deer-hair Fry

Brown trout

Rainbow trout

Although not an easy pattern to tie, if the correct techniques are mastered first, the Deer-hair Fry is well within the skill level of most tyers. The key is to come to grips with spinning deer hair. Once the basic technique for tying a Muddler has been understood, it is simply a matter of expanding the process to cover the whole of the hook shank. It is important to add hair in even bunches, and to pack each spun bunch against the previous, so that the consistency of the hair is the same from the bend to the eye. That achieved, it is a matter of trimming the hair to produce a basic fish shape. The color is applied by blending gray and olive waterproof markers together, either with the fingertips or with a piece of paper towel. The decal eyes are attached with a spot of epoxy resin worked into the hair.

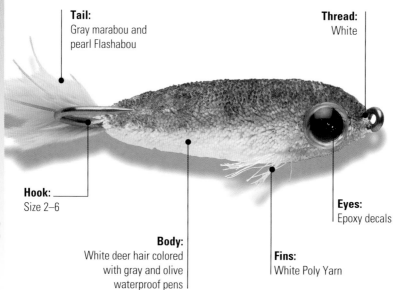

Tail:
Gray marabou and
pearl Flashabou

Thread:
White

Hook:
Size 2–6

Eyes:
Epoxy decals

Body:
White deer hair colored
with gray and olive
waterproof pens

Fins:
White Poly Yarn

1 Fix the hook in the vise and run the tying thread on at the eye. Carry it down the shank in close turns, stopping at a point opposite the barb. Catch in a tuft of gray marabou and a few strands of pearl Flashabou.

2 Cut a large bunch of white deer hair from the skin and catch it in just in front of the tail using three loose turns of thread. Pull the thread tight, causing the hair to flare.

3 Continue adding turns of thread through the hair, at the same time easing it around the hook shank so that it is evenly distributed. Pull the hair back toward the tail and fix it in place by winding the thread in front.

4 Add further bunches of deer hair in the same manner, packing each bunch back against the previous one to produce a dense effect. With about three-quarters of the shank covered, catch in a length of white Poly Yarn.

5 Add one last bunch of deer hair in front of the yarn so that the whole of the shank is covered. Cast off the tying thread with a whip finish and begin trimming the hair into a basic fish shape. Remember not to trim off the yarn.

6 Trim the hair with increasingly smaller cuts until the body is smooth. Stick eyes on both sides of the head with epoxy resin. Finally, color the top of the body with gray and olive waterproof pens, blending them together with the fingertips.

Missionary

Brown trout

Rainbow trout

This version of the Missionary was designed by the late Dick Shrive to act as a baitfish imitation that could be fished very slowly. The way that the wing is applied is the key to the pattern's action. Rather than simply being tied in as a bunch of fibers, the gray mallard flank feather is used whole. With the fibers at the base removed, to leave a spoon-shaped feather a little longer than the body and tail combined, the prepared wing is tied on flat to the top of the hook. This allows the wing to act like a parachute, slowing down the Missionary's descent through the water. The pattern is often taken on the drop because it flutters toward the lakebed after being cast. This white and red combination is the original, and a version that uses a dyed yellow mallard flank feather plus yellow chenille is also very effective.

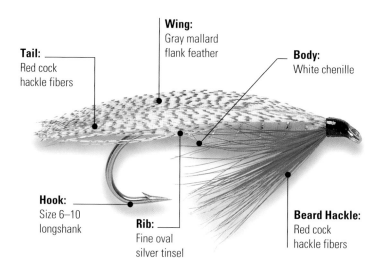

Wing:
Gray mallard
flank feather

Tail:
Red cock
hackle fibers

Body:
White chenille

Hook:
Size 6–10
longshank

Rib:
Fine oval
silver tinsel

Beard Hackle:
Red cock
hackle fibers

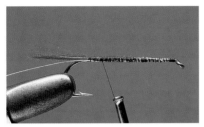

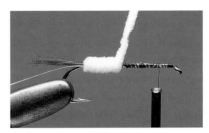

1 Fix the hook and run the thread to the bend. Catch in a tail of red cock hackle fibers and 3 inches (7.5cm) of fine, oval, silver tinsel. Double the waste end of the tinsel back on itself. Wind the thread over the ends and return it to the bend.

2 Take a length of white chenille and, from one end, remove a short section of the herl to expose the core. Catch it in by the core, then wind the chenille along the shank in touching turns. Using hackle pliers can prevent soiling the chenille.

3 At the eye, secure the chenille with thread and trim the waste end with scissors.

4 Wind the tinsel over the body in open, evenly spaced turns. Secure the loose end just behind the eye and remove the excess.

5 Add a beard hackle of red cock hackle fibers to the underside of the eye. Allow the hackle fibers to flare slightly around the sides of the body. Select a spoon-shaped gray mallard flank feather and remove the fibers from the base.

6 Position the feather flat over the body and catch it in with turns of thread over the feather stem. Pull the stem so the feather is drawn forward and wraps around the body. Secure with thread and snip off the excess stem. Build a head and cast off.

201

Booby

The buoyant eyes of the Booby allow it to be fished on the surface, on a floating line, or deep down, near the lakebed, with a fast-sinking line and a short leader. The eyes were originally formed from two polystyrene balls wrapped in stocking mesh. However, these balls were easily crushed and their buoyancy diminished. Using a section of microcellular plastic foam alleviates the problem, because this type of foam is far tougher and can be fixed directly to the hook with tying thread. To make the eyes, a foam block can be cut to shape. Alternatively, foam dowel is now available and only needs the ends trimming to the right shape.

Brown trout

Rainbow trout

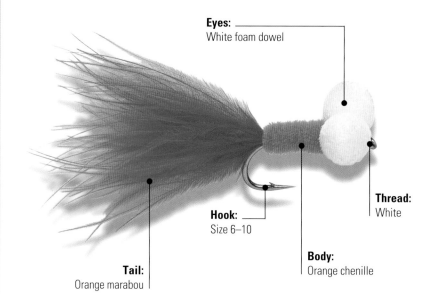

Eyes: White foam dowel

Thread: White

Hook: Size 6–10

Body: Orange chenille

Tail: Orange marabou

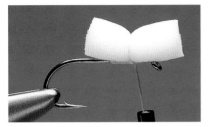

1 Having fixed the hook in the vise, run the tying thread on at the eye and wind on a few touching turns to form a solid base. Catch in a section of white foam dowel with thread wraps wound at its middle.

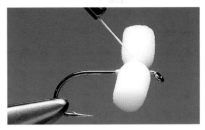

2 Twist the foam dowel so that it lies across the shank rather than along it. Secure it in position with figure-of-eight turns of tying thread.

3 Cast off the tying thread with a whip finish. Using a sharp, pointed pair of scissors, make repeated small cuts to the ends of the foam dowel to form round eyes.

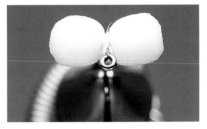

4 Check the look of the eyes from all angles and aim to form two round shapes of equal size. Run a drop of Super Glue between the eyes and allow it to dry.

5 Run the tying thread back on behind the eyes and wind it down to the bend. Take a generous pinch of orange marabou and secure it in place with tight thread wraps.

6 Prepare 2 inches (5cm) of orange chenille by exposing a short section of the core. Catch it in at the base of the tail by the core. Wind the chenille right up to the eyes, secure, and remove the excess. Cast off.

203

Mrs. Simpson

Brown trout

Rainbow trout

This New Zealand pattern makes a great representation of something big and meaty found on the bottom of either rivers or lakes—anything from a small fish to a dragonfly nymph, even a crayfish, at a pinch. Because it is designed to fish deep, it is invariably tied with an underbody of lead wire, over which are wound turns of water-absorbent chenille in various colors. The wing, however, is the most interesting part of this fly, comprising overlapping layers of rump feathers taken from a cock ring-necked pheasant. Sometimes known as church windows, due to their patterning, these feathers are fixed to the sides of the body rather than to the top and bottom.

Weight:
Lead wire

Body:
Red chenille

Wing:
Cock ring-necked pheasant
rump feathers

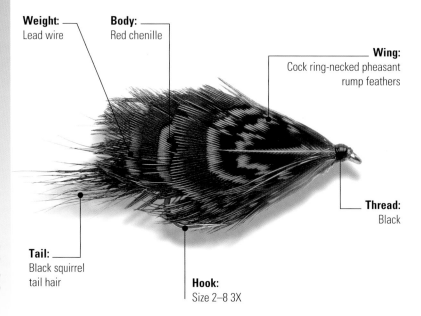

Thread:
Black

Tail:
Black squirrel
tail hair

Hook:
Size 2–8 3X

1 Fix the hook in the vise and wind on close turns of lead wire, leaving a short bare section of shank to the front and rear. Secure in place with tying thread and catch in a tuft of black squirrel tail hair as the tail.

2 Take 3 inches (7.5cm) of red chenille and prepare it by exposing a short section of the core from one end. Catch in the chenille at the base of the tail, using the bare core section, and wind it over the lead wire.

3 Secure the chenille close to the eye and trim the excess. Select a feather from the saddle-patch of a male ring-necked pheasant. Strip away the waste fibers from the base to leave a section of bare stem.

4 Prepare a second, identically sized feather in the same way. Catch the feathers in on both sides of the body so that the tips project a short distance past the end of the hook.

5 Prepare another pair of feathers and secure them in place on both sides of the first two. They should be staggered so that the tips of the second fall slightly short of the first.

6 Select a third and final pair of feathers and apply them in the same way as before. Secure in place with tight thread turns and remove the waste hackle stems. Complete by forming a small, neat head and cast off.

Sparkler

Brown
trout

Rainbow
trout

Although it vaguely resembles a small baitfish, the Sparkler is
tied as an out-and-out attractor. It is most effective when fished
on a fast-sinking line, especially when targeting rainbow trout in
lakes. During the summer months, these fish can often be found
feeding a few feet down on vast clouds of tiny water fleas
known as Daphnia. Though these creatures are impossible to
imitate, because of their size and sheer numbers, trout are more
than willing to grab a flashy pattern such as the Sparkler when
it is retrieved past them. The Sparkler is made up entirely of
manmade products, from its wing and tail of metallic plastic
tinsel to the chunky body formed from a material sold under
brand names such as Fritz, Cactus Chenille, and Ersatz.

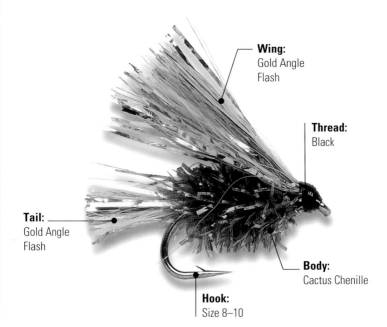

Wing:
Gold Angle
Flash

Thread:
Black

Tail:
Gold Angle
Flash

Body:
Cactus Chenille

Hook:
Size 8–10

1 Fix the hook in the vise and run the tying thread on at the eye. Carry the thread down the shank to a point opposite the barb. Catch in strands of gold Angle Flash.

2 Fix the Angle Flash in place before winding the thread over the waste ends along the shank. Take a length of Cactus Chenille and remove a short section of the sparkling herl to expose the central core.

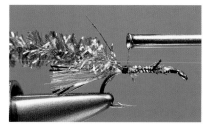 

3 At the base of the tail, catch the Cactus Chenille in place by winding tight turns of thread over the exposed core. If this isn't done, an unsightly bulge will form at the tail.

4 Grasp the end of the Cactus Chenille with a pair of hackle pliers. Twist the chenille to flare the herl, then wind it toward the eye in close turns.

5 Stop winding the chenille a short distance from the eye. Secure the loose end before removing the excess. Take a bunch of gold Angle Flash twice the length of the intended wing and catch it in place halfway along its length.

6 Fold the Angle Flash over the eye and back over the wing so that its density is doubled. Secure the wing with thread wraps and trim the ends so that they are level with those of the tail. Build a neat head before casting off the thread.

207

CHAPTER FIVE

HAIRWINGS

Hairwings, or bucktails, are usually tied quite large, either as general attractor patterns or to imitate a range of small- to medium-sized baitfish. The particular advantage of using hair as a winging material is that it is tough and well able to stand up to heavy fishing. In fast-flowing water, hair provides enough mobility to give the fly the necessary "life," while its slight stiffness prevents the wing from becoming flattened or getting wrapped around the hook bend.

Hair is extremely versatile and found in a range of natural and dyed colors. For large patterns the tail of the white-tailed deer is most widely used, either plain or dyed, while for small- to medium-sized flies gray squirrel tail or calf tail are the most popular alternatives. Although bucktail is still one of the most commonly used types of hair, other softer hairs are also used. Arctic fox is a particular favorite because it is soft and mobile, and can be obtained in all the popular colors.

Due to the robustness of hair and ease of tying, it has become the favored material for winging many patterns. In fact, most modern salmon patterns use hair rather than feathers, and even a number of traditional feather-winged patterns used for Atlantic salmon have been converted into hairwings.

Apart from tying it as a bunch at the eye, hair can also be used in other ways. One very popular method is in the Zonker style of winging, where the skin that supports the hair is cut into thin strips and secured along the body. This way, a long, mobile effect is created, combining both the wing and tail. Rabbit and mink hair are the best materials for this style of tying.

Mickey Finn

This gaudy hairwing is a great attractor fly. The combination of red and yellow bucktail in the wing can often tempt fish that have shunned more somber-colored flies. Various types of silver tinsel can be used for the body of the Mickey Finn, but in this case Mylar tubing is the chosen material. It is very tough, and, being plastic, doesn't tarnish. Mylar tubing also has an attractive scale pattern formed by the weave of the strands, and works well for both attractor patterns and those designed to imitate small fish.

Arctic
char

Cutthroat

Rainbow
trout

Coho
salmon

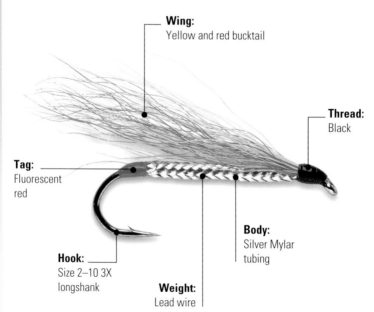

Wing:
Yellow and red bucktail

Thread:
Black

Tag:
Fluorescent
red

Hook:
Size 2–10 3X
longshank

Weight:
Lead wire

Body:
Silver Mylar
tubing

1 Starting from a third of the way down the shank, wind on close turns of lead wire. Cover the lead with fluorescent red tying thread, stopping opposite the barb. Cut a section of silver Mylar tubing one-and-a-half times the hook length.

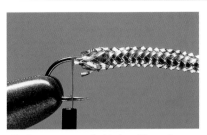

2 Remove any core inside the tubing and compress it slightly to increase the inside diameter. Slide the tubing along the shank up to the tying thread.

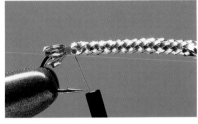

3 Allow the frayed ends of the tubing to slide slightly past where the thread is resting. Secure the end of the tubing in place with turns of thread.

4 Carefully trim off the excess frayed ends of Mylar, then cover the rear of the body with tying thread to form a tag. Cast off the thread with a whip finish and apply a coat of clear lacquer.

5 Attach black tying thread at the eye. Pull the Mylar tubing forward so it is tight on the hook, and secure the loose end with thread. Trim away the excess.

6 Take a pinch of dyed red bucktail and sandwich it between two bunches of yellow bucktail. Catch the hair in at the eye to form the wing. Build a neat head and cast off the thread.

Polar Shrimp

Coho
salmon

Steelhead

This brightly colored fly is a great favorite both for steelhead and
the various species of Pacific salmon. The body is formed either
from wool or chenille, the latter giving a more translucent effect.
The white wing can be formed from either calf or polar bear
hair. As when tying all hairwinged flies, care must be taken to
ensure that the wing is securely locked in place. Use a strong
thread that is not too thick. The more turns that can be applied
to the wing base, the more likely it is to hold. As an additional
precaution, after the first few positioning thread wraps have
been made, a drop of clear lacquer can be applied and allowed
to soak in.

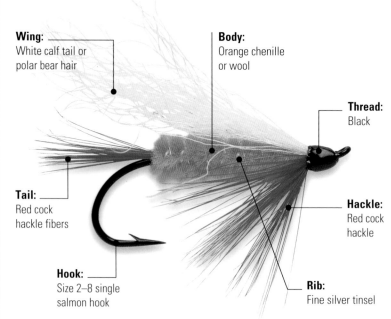

Wing:
White calf tail or
polar bear hair

Body:
Orange chenille
or wool

Thread:
Black

Tail:
Red cock
hackle fibers

Hackle:
Red cock
hackle

Hook:
Size 2–8 single
salmon hook

Rib:
Fine silver tinsel

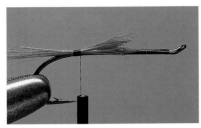

1 Once the hook is fixed in the vise, wind the tying thread in close turns over the loop eye. Carry it down the shank and catch in a few fibers of dyed red cock hackle.

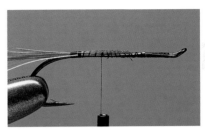

2 At the same point, catch in 3 inches (7.5cm) of fine, silver tinsel. Secure the waste ends along the shank with thread, helping to form an even base for the body.

3 Remove some of the fibers from the end of a 3-inch (7.5-cm) length of fluorescent orange chenille. Catch the chenille in at the base of the tail, using the bare section of core. Wind it along the shank in closely butted turns.

4 Stop the chenille just short of the eye. Wind on the silver tinsel in evenly spaced turns. Secure and remove the excess chenille and tinsel. Add three full turns of red cock hackle.

5 Secure the hackle tip with thread and remove the excess. Stroke the hackle fibers back along and beneath the body. Fix in position with thread turns.

6 Remove a pinch of polar bear hair from the skin. Catch the hair in at the eye with tight thread wraps. Add a drop of lacquer to help secure the hair. Cast off.

213

Clouser Minnow

The Clouser Minnow is an extremely effective baitfish imitation that catches a whole range of game fish in fresh- and saltwater. Its allure comes from a combination of heavy lead eyes and long, mobile tail and wing that give it a wonderful ducking-diving action on every twitch of the retrieve. It is also tied to take the knocks that come when catching large, powerful fish, and the use of tough materials such as bucktail, ultra-strong thread, and Super Glue ensures that the Clouser is very robust. It is an easy pattern to tie: The body consists of simple, crossed-thread wraps over the waste ends of the tailing materials. Also, because the pattern is tied to fish point-up, to avoid snagging the bottom, the heavy lead eyes are tied on top of the shank rather than underneath.

Brown
trout

Arctic
char

Rainbow
trout

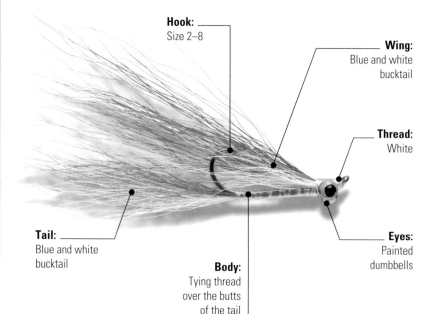

Hook:
Size 2–8

Wing:
Blue and white
bucktail

Thread:
White

Eyes:
Painted
dumbbells

Body:
Tying thread
over the butts
of the tail

Tail:
Blue and white
bucktail

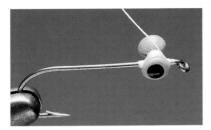

1 Once the hook is fixed in the vise, run the tying thread on at the eye. Wind on a number of thread wraps to build up a solid base, then use figure-of-eight thread wraps to secure painted dumbbell eyes in place on top of the shank.

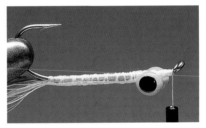

2 Wind the thread, in touching turns, down to the bend and back to the eyes. Take a slim bunch each of blue and white bucktail and catch them in at the eyes to form a tail. Wind the thread in tight, open turns over the ends of the bucktail.

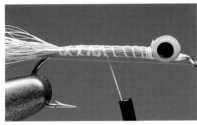

3 Carry the thread down to the hook bend and back to the eyes. These crossed turns of thread will lock the tail in position.

4 Carry the thread right up to the hook's eye, then invert the hook in the vise so that it is sitting point-up.

5 Take two more bunches of blue and white bucktail and place them together. Catch them in at the hook's eye so that their tips are level with those of the tail.

6 Build a neat head. Carry the thread behind the dumbbell eyes and use very tight wraps to lock the wing in place. Cast off the thread and run a drop of Super Glue into the thread wraps holding the wing and eyes.

215

Thunder Creek Silver Shiner

Brown trout

Arctic char

Cutthroat

One of a large group of themed patterns, the Thunder Creek Silver Shiner makes a robust and effective imitation of a small baitfish. Although it looks simple, it is not that easy to tie because getting the hair the right length and keeping the two colors separate takes a reasonable level of tying skill. The Thunder Creek range was devised by American tyer Keith Fulsher to imitate a whole variety of fish species, and the Silver Shiner is one of the simplest. Once the wing has been swept back and secured in position, the head should be coated with layers of clear varnish or a single application of clear epoxy resin. When dry, a white eye with a black pupil can be painted on each side of the head.

Rainbow trout

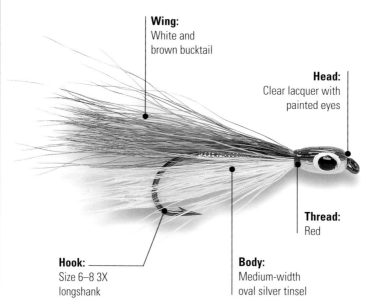

Wing:
White and brown bucktail

Head:
Clear lacquer with painted eyes

Thread:
Red

Hook:
Size 6–8 3X longshank

Body:
Medium-width oval silver tinsel

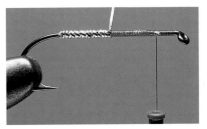

1 After fixing the hook in the vise, run on the tying thread at the eye and carry it down the shank to the bend. Catch in 6 inches (15cm) of embossed or medium-width, oval, silver tinsel.

2 Wind the thread on in close turns to lock the waste end of the tinsel along the shank. This provides an even base for the tinsel body. Wind the tinsel in touching turns toward the eye.

3 Secure the end of the tinsel close to the eye and remove the excess. Take a bunch of white bucktail, approximately twice the length of the hook, and catch it in under the eye so the tips project past it.

4 Take a bunch of brown bucktail the same length as the white. Catch it in on the upper side of the shank so the tips of both bunches are level. Secure the butts with tight, close turns of tying thread.

5 Carry the thread a quarter of the way back down the shank. Draw both bunches of hair back over the body, taking care not to mix the two colors too much. Secure them in place with thread wraps.

6 Cast off the tying thread with a whip finish to leave a conspicuous red collar. Apply two coats of clear lacquer to the head and, when dry, add painted eyes on each side.

217

Garry

Atlantic salmon

Tied on small sized hooks, from a 6 down to a 10, the Garry is a great fly for summer salmon, as the river clears after a summer spate. Tied large, either on a longshanked double hook, as a tube fly, or on a Waddington shank, it is also extremely effective both in the spring and the fall when the river is running high and slightly colored. Its wing is constructed from dyed yellow hair with a few fibers of dyed red hair underneath: a striking combination that contrasts well with the black floss body and blue throat hackle. The type of hair used depends on the size of the fly being tied. Bucktail is the usual choice when using big hooks and Waddingtons, while the softer, finer fibers of squirrel tail work better on small hooks.

Tail:
Golden pheasant
crest feather

Wing:
Dyed yellow and
dyed red bucktail

Thread:
Black

Tag:
Fine oval silver
tinsel and golden
yellow floss

Hackle:
Dyed blue guinea
fowl feather fibers

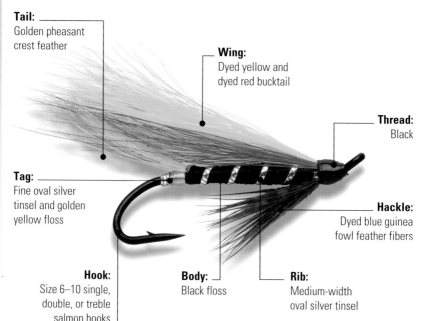

Hook:
Size 6–10 single,
double, or treble
salmon hooks

Body:
Black floss

Rib:
Medium-width
oval silver tinsel

1 Fix the hook and run the thread down the shank to opposite the barb. Wind on a tag of fine, oval, silver tinsel, then catch in 2 inches (5cm) of golden yellow floss. Wind the floss in front of the tinsel securing the loose end with thread.

2 Remove the loose end of the floss then prepare and catch in a tail of golden pheasant crest feather. Next, take 3 inches (7.5cm) of medium-width, oval, silver tinsel and catch it in at the base of the tail.

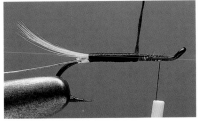

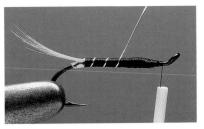

3 Take 4 inches (10cm) of black floss and catch it in at the tail base so that the waste end lies along the length of the hook shank. Wind the tying thread up to the eye, then follow it with close turns of floss.

4 Carry the floss right up to the tying thread to form a smooth tapering body. Secure and remove the loose end of floss before winding the silver tinsel over it in open, evenly spaced turns.

5 With the tinsel rib in place, secure the end with thread and remove the excess. Prepare a bunch of dyed blue guinea fowl feather fibers, and making sure that the tips are level, catch them in under the hook shank to form a beard hackle.

6 Prepare a bunch of dyed yellow bucktail removing the damaged hairs. Add a few fibers of dyed red bucktail underneath and catch in the hair as a wing so the tip is level with that of the tail. Secure in place with tight thread turns and cast off.

219

HAIRWINGS

Munro Killer

Atlantic
salmon

Many hairwinged salmon flies, particularly those tied on standard
single or double hooks, have quite short wings, often reaching
only as far as the hook bend. The Munro Killer breaks this rule,
and has a wing at least twice the length of the hook. The result
is a fly with far more action in the water, making it effective even
in slower moving parts of a river. The Munro Killer also has a
bicolored wing formed by overlaying yellow bucktail with black
bucktail. The two colors are placed together before tying in so
that the bunches blend together slightly. The hackle comprises a
swept back orange wet-fly hackle, over which contrasting fibers
of dyed blue guinea fowl are laid. Incidentally, blue guinea fowl
is often used on large flies as a substitute for blue jay.

Wing:
Yellow and black
bucktail

Rib:
Oval gold tinsel

Thread:
Black

Hook:
Size 4–8 single or
double salmon hooks

Body:
Black floss

Hackle:
Dyed orange cock
hackle and dyed
blue guinea fowl

Tag:
Fine gold
tinsel

220

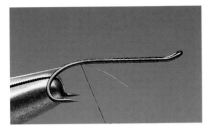

1 Fix the hook in the vise. If using a double hook the jaws will need to be angled so the shank is parallel to the tyer. Run the tying thread from the eye to where the two hooks divide. Catch in 2 inches (5cm) of fine, gold tinsel.

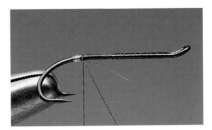

2 Wind the thread a short distance back up the shank. Take hold of the tinsel and wind on five or six turns to form a tag. Secure the loose end of the tinsel with tying thread.

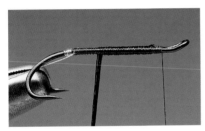

3 Catch in 3 inches (7.5cm) of oval, gold tinsel in front of the tag. Wind the thread up to the eye, covering the waste ends of both tinsels. Catch in a length of black floss behind the eye and wind it down to the tag in close turns.

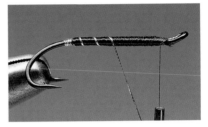

4 Wind the floss back to its catching-in point to create a double layer. Secure the loose end with thread and remove. Wind on five evenly spaced turns of the oval, gold tinsel to form the rib. Secure the loose end and remove any excess.

5 Prepare a dyed orange cock hackle and catch it in by the stem just in front of the body. Wind on three turns, then use the thread to position the hackle fibers so that they sweep back along and below the shank. Trim the excess hackle.

6 Catch in a few fibers of dyed blue guinea fowl in front of the orange hackle. Take a small bunch each of yellow and black bucktail. Lay the black on top and catch both in at the eye. This wing should be twice the length of the hook. Cast off.

221

Stoat's Tail

Atlantic
salmon

Sea trout

A jet-black dressing contrasted with a sparkling silver rib and a
bright tail of golden pheasant crest feather make the Stoat's Tail
one of the most effective of Atlantic salmon flies. The dark
silhouette it creates works in all conditions, from the colored
water of a spring flood to the crystal-clear flow of a river at
summer level. Originally, real stoat's tail was used for the wing,
but now dyed bucktail is preferred, or squirrel tail in the smaller
sizes of hook. The floss body can be made with traditional silk
floss or manmade rayon. The latter spreads particularly well,
creating a nice smooth finish. The only drawback is that the very
fine rayon fibers are prone to snagging when being wound. To
avoid this, load the bobbin into a holder and wind the floss with
the spigot tube so the fingers never touch it.

Tail:
Golden pheasant
crest feather

Body:
Black rayon floss

Wing:
Dyed black squirrel tail hair

Thread:
Black

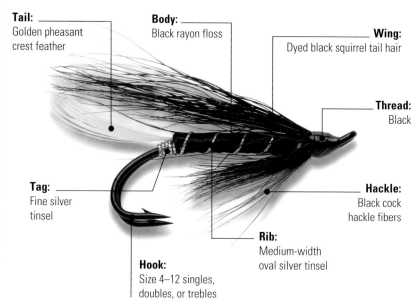

Tag:
Fine silver
tinsel

Hackle:
Black cock
hackle fibers

Rib:
Medium-width
oval silver tinsel

Hook:
Size 4–12 singles,
doubles, or trebles

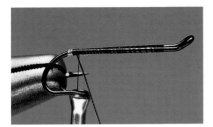

1 Secure the hook in the vise and run the thread from the eye to where the hooks separate. Catch in 2 inches (5cm) of fine, silver tinsel. Run the thread a short way back up the shank, then wind on four turns of tinsel as a tag.

2 Secure the loose end of the tinsel and trim the excess. Next, catch in a tail of golden pheasant crest feather and 3 inches (7.5cm) of medium-width, oval, silver tinsel.

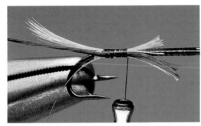

3 At the same point, catch in a length of black rayon floss whose spool is held in a bobbin holder. Allow the waste ends of all the materials to lie along the shank.

4 Wind the tying thread over all the waste ends to form an even base for the body. Stop the thread a short distance from the eye. Take hold of the bobbin holder and wind the floss evenly along the shank.

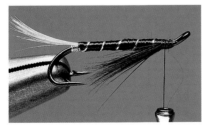

5 Secure the loose end of the floss and remove any excess materials. Wind the tinsel in open, evenly spaced turns over the floss body. Secure and trim the wastage. Add a beard hackle of black cock hackle fibers.

6 Take a bunch of dyed black squirrel tail hair and remove any broken fibers. The tips need to be level with the tail. Trim off the excess hair at the butts and secure the wing in place with tight thread wraps. Cast off.

223

Blue Charm

Atlantic
salmon

Sea trout

The Blue Charm is a standard Atlantic salmon fly, effective
throughout the summer months, when the river is running at its
normal level. This version is tied as a simple hairwing, rather than
the original that uses strips of bronze mallard edged with barred
teal. Hairwing flies are now the most popular type of salmon fly
because they are easier to tie and more robust than their
feather-winged equivalents. When tying floss bodies, using a
double layer helps to create a smoother effect than a single
layer. The pattern works best tied on either single or double
hooks in sizes 4–10, and in its smallest sizes is very effective
when night fishing for sea trout.

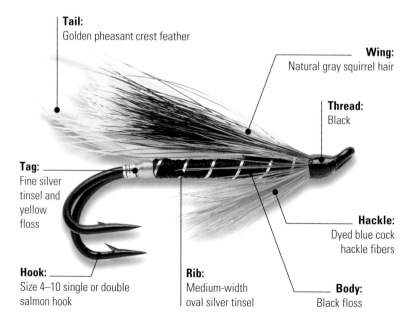

Tail:
Golden pheasant crest feather

Wing:
Natural gray squirrel hair

Thread:
Black

Tag:
Fine silver
tinsel and
yellow
floss

Hackle:
Dyed blue cock
hackle fibers

Hook:
Size 4–10 single or double
salmon hook

Rib:
Medium-width
oval silver tinsel

Body:
Black floss

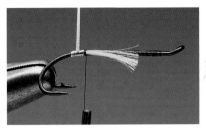

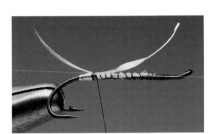

1 Fix the hook in the vise with the shank parallel to the tyer. Wind the thread to where the two hooks divide and catch in 2 inches (5cm) of silver tinsel. Run the thread a short way back up the shank, then wind on four turns of tinsel as a tag.

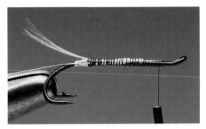

2 Secure the loose end of the tinsel and remove. Catch in 2 inches (5cm) of yellow floss, a short distance in front of the tag, and wind it down to the tag and back. Ensure that the floss spreads as it is wound so that the effect is as smooth as possible.

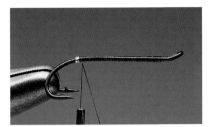

3 Wind the thread over the waste ends of the floss to form an even base for the body. Take the thread back to the floss tag and catch in a tail of golden pheasant crest feather. Choose a feather that is brightly colored and has a nice sparkle.

4 Take 3 inches (7.5cm) of medium-width, oval, silver tinsel and catch it in at the tail. Wind the thread over the waste ends of feather and tinsel then back to the eye.

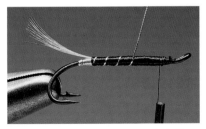

5 Catch in a length of black floss and wind it down to the tail and back to form a smooth body. Secure the loose end of floss and remove the excess. Wind on five, evenly spaced turns of tinsel as the rib.

6 Secure the tinsel and remove any waste. Trim a beard hackle of dyed blue cock hackle fibers so that they fall short of the hook points and catch in. Next, catch in a wing of natural gray squirrel hair so that the tips are level with the tail. Cast off.

225

Silver Rat

Atlantic salmon

One of a series of highly effective salmon flies, the Silver Rat is a great pattern at times when the river is running low and clear. Its fine, mobile wing is formed by a thin bunch of gray fox hair. The hair of the gray fox is extremely fine, so it is a good idea to leave a small proportion of the softer underfur still in place to increase the density at the wing base. The hair is smooth, so gripping it with the tying thread can be a problem. To stop the hair from coming out, special locking turns are made around the wing base. These turns are made just around the hair and are covered with further normal thread wraps, plus the hackle.

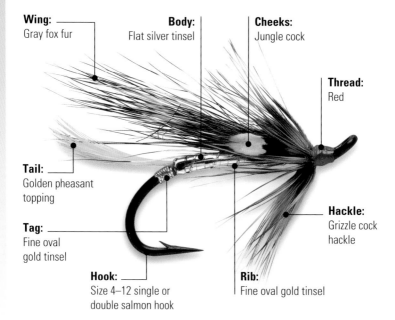

Wing:
Gray fox fur

Body:
Flat silver tinsel

Cheeks:
Jungle cock

Thread:
Red

Tail:
Golden pheasant topping

Tag:
Fine oval gold tinsel

Hackle:
Grizzle cock hackle

Hook:
Size 4–12 single or double salmon hook

Rib:
Fine oval gold tinsel

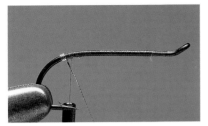

1 Fix the hook in the vise and run on the thread at the eye. Carry it down the shank to a point opposite the barb. Catch in 2 inches (5cm) of fine, oval, gold tinsel and wind on five turns to form a tag. Secure with thread and remove the excess.

2 Select a golden pheasant topping feather, ensuring that the color is clear and that there are no damaged fibers. Catch it in so that it forms an upward-curving tail.

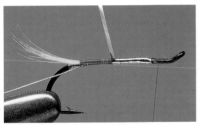

3 Catch in 3 inches (7.5cm) of fine, oval, gold tinsel and wind the thread over its waste end and that of the topping feather to form a smooth base for the body. Catch in 4 inches (10cm) of flat, silver tinsel and wind in touching turns to the tail.

4 Wind the silver tinsel back to its catching-in point. Rib the body with evenly spaced turns of the oval, gold tinsel. Take a pinch of gray fox fur and secure at the eye with thread turns. Wind a few locking turns around the wing base.

5 Remove any excess hair at the eye with fine-tipped scissors. Add further tight thread wraps for extra security, then apply a couple of slightly looser turns at the wing base for position.

6 Add a cheek of jungle cock to either side of the wing. Select a soft-fibered grizzle cock hackle and catch it in at the base of the wing. Wind on three turns of the hackle to form a collar. Secure the tip with thread and remove the excess.

Ally's Shrimp

Atlantic
salmon

Scottish salmon angler Alistair Gowans developed this particular
version of the Shrimp Fly, which incorporates a long, mobile tail.
So effective has it been that it is probably the number one fly
for Atlantic salmon in use today. The original was tied with long
fibers of orange bucktail projecting from the hook bend. These
not only imitate the whiskers of a real shrimp, but also give
the fly an action that summer salmon find difficult to resist.
Although the Ally's Shrimp was first tied just in orange, the style
has proved so effective that other colors are now widely used,
including red, yellow, and purple. The recipe for this pattern
stipulates a red head that can be formed using red tying thread
or by adding a drop of red varnish.

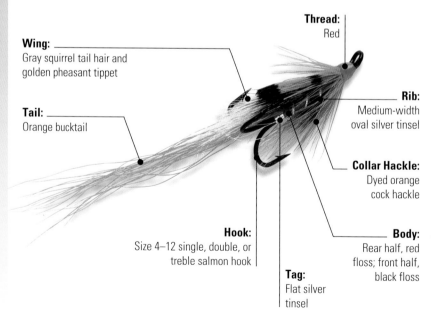

Thread:
Red

Wing:
Gray squirrel tail hair and
golden pheasant tippet

Rib:
Medium-width
oval silver tinsel

Tail:
Orange bucktail

Collar Hackle:
Dyed orange
cock hackle

Hook:
Size 4–12 single, double, or
treble salmon hook

Body:
Rear half, red
floss; front half,
black floss

Tag:
Flat silver
tinsel

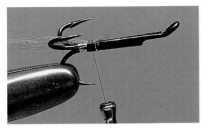

1 Fix the hook with the eye pointing upward, and run the thread along the shank. Catch in 2 inches (5cm) of flat, silver tinsel. Run the thread a short way up the shank, then wind on four turns of tinsel. Catch in a slim tail of orange bucktail.

2 At the base of the tail catch in 3 inches (7.5cm) of medium-width, oval, silver tinsel. Carry the thread halfway back up the shank and catch in a length of red floss. Wind it to the tail and back to form the rear half of the body.

3 Secure and remove the waste end of floss, then carry the thread up to the eye. Catch in a length of black floss and wind it down to the red section and back. Wind five turns of the oval tinsel over both sections, secure, and trim the excess.

4 Select a bunch of gray squirrel tail hair. Divide it in two and attach one half below and one half above the body. The tips of the hair should project just past the bends of the hooks. Lock the hair in place with tight turns of thread.

5 Select a large golden pheasant tippet feather. Trim the base so that the tippets are just longer than the hook shank and catch them in over the top of the upper wing.

6 Prepare a dyed orange cock hackle and catch it in by the stem at the eye. Grasp the tip with hackle pliers and wind on three turns. Stroke the fibers back over the body and secure in place with turns of thread. Trim the excess hackle and cast off.

229

HAIRWINGS

Zonker

In its basic gray and silver form, the Zonker makes a fine representation of a range of baitfish species. However, it may be tied in a wide range of colors from black, white, and orange to purple, the latter being very effective for various species of Pacific salmon. Whatever the color, the technique for tying the Zonker is the same, employing a braided Mylar tubing for the body over which is stretched a strip of rabbit fur still on the skin. When cutting rabbit strip in this way, it is important to use a sharp blade and always cut from the skin side to prevent damaging the hair. Depending on the size of hook being used, the fur strip should be ⅛–³⁄₁₆ inch (3–5mm) wide.

Brown trout

Arctic char

Rainbow trout

Coho salmon

Chinook salmon

Wing and Tail:
A strip of rabbit fur still on the skin

Hackle:
Grizzle cock hackle

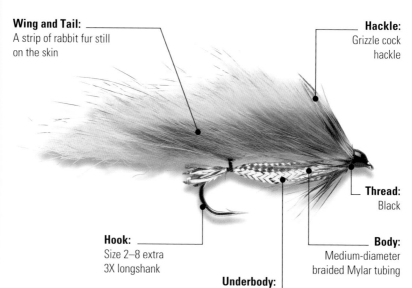

Thread:
Black

Hook:
Size 2–8 extra 3X longshank

Underbody:
Self-adhesive foil

Body:
Medium-diameter braided Mylar tubing

230

1 Fix the hook in the vise and cut a section of self-adhesive foil a little shorter than the length of the shank. Fold the foil over the shank and press the surfaces together so that they stick.

2 Using scissors, trim the foil under the hook to form a basic fish shape. Run the tips of the scissors along the underneath of the shank to stop the foil springing apart.

3 Cast on the tying thread at the end of the foil underbody, opposite the barb. Take 2 inches (5cm) of medium-diameter, braided Mylar tubing and remove the central core. Slip the braid over the eye and ease it along the body.

4 Allow the ends of the braid to fray a little. Push these ends past the bend and secure the tubing in place with turns of tying thread. Cast off the tying thread at this point.

5 Run the thread back on at the eye. Pull the tubing tight and secure it with the thread. Trim off the excess Mylar at the eye. Take 2 inches (5cm) of rabbit fur, still on the skin, and catch it in at the eye.

6 Remove the excess skin strip at the eye before applying a collar of grizzle cock hackle. Build a neat head and cast off. Run the thread back on at the end of the body and secure the rear end of the rabbit strip. Cast off again.

231

Minkie

While some bait imitations might look more natural, there are few that match the fish-catching ability of the Minkie. When trout are feeding hard on small fish, this pattern will outfish almost all others, the key to its success being a highly mobile wing of mink strip. Mink is shorter in fiber than rabbit, which allows a much slimmer effect to be produced; and because it has plenty of built-in action, this pattern can be fished very slowly. All too often trout that crash headlong with explosive force into shoals of baitfish will actually prefer to take a slow moving fly.

Brown trout

Rainbow trout

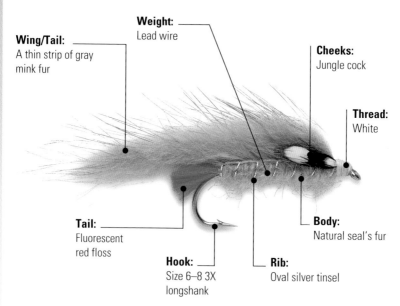

Weight:
Lead wire

Wing/Tail:
A thin strip of gray mink fur

Cheeks:
Jungle cock

Thread:
White

Tail:
Fluorescent red floss

Hook:
Size 6–8 3X longshank

Rib:
Oval silver tinsel

Body:
Natural seal's fur

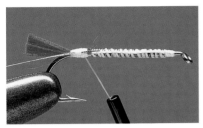

1 Fix the hook and wind on close turns of lead wire. Stop opposite the hook point, leaving a small gap to the bend. Run on the tying thread and cover the lead wire. Tie in a tail of folded strands of floss, plus 3 inches (7.5cm) of oval, silver tinsel.

2 Take a large pinch of seal's fur and apply it to the thread. Dub it on to create a thick rope and wind it over the turns of lead wire.

3 Using a scalpel blade, cut a strip of mink fur 2 inches (5cm) long and ⅛ inch (3mm) wide. Catch it in at the eye with tight thread wraps. Trim off the excess at the eye.

4 Moisten the mink strip and stretch it along the top of the body. Divide the hair at the tail and make one turn with the tinsel. Continue working the tinsel through the wing in the same way, dividing the hair as you go.

5 Secure the tinsel at the eye. Using a pair of scissors, remove the loose end of tinsel.

6 Add short jungle cock cheeks to both sides of the wing. Build a neat head and cast off.

Egg-sucking Leech

This is the pattern to go for if you want a big, heavy fly for catching chinook salmon. It uses rabbit strip for both the tail and the body hackle, and combined with a heavily weighted underbody it literally pulses with life on every twitch of the retrieve. When using rabbit strip, where the hair is still attached, the trick is to choose a section of pelt with thin and pliable skin. This allows a narrow strip to be wound as a hackle so that the hair lies sloping back along the body. The strip of skin used should be ⅛–³⁄₁₆ inch (3–5mm) wide, and always cut on the skin side with a sharp blade to prevent damaging the hair.

Brown
trout

Arctic
char

Rainbow
trout

Coho
salmon

Chinook
salmon

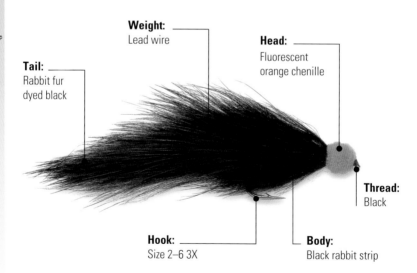

Weight:
Lead wire

Head:
Fluorescent
orange chenille

Tail:
Rabbit fur
dyed black

Thread:
Black

Hook:
Size 2–6 3X

Body:
Black rabbit strip

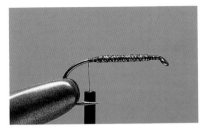

1 Fix the hook in the vise. Starting behind the eye, cover three-quarters of the shank with touching turns of lead wire. Secure the wire by running over it with tying thread turns, starting at the eye and stopping a little past the lead body.

2 Cut a strip of rabbit fur 2 inches (5cm) long and ⅛ inch (3mm) wide. Secure the strip of rabbit fur in place, skin-side down, in the gap left behind the lead body, opposite the barb.

3 Cut a second, slightly longer, strip of fur. Check which direction the fur is lying and catch the strip in by its rear end, at the same place as the first strip.

4 With the fingers or a pair of hackle pliers, take hold of the second fur strip and wind it in touching turns up to the eye. Stroke the hair back after each turn. Secure the loose end of the fur strip and remove the excess.

5 Take 2 inches (5cm) of fluorescent orange chenille and expose a short length of the core from one end. Use the bare section of core to catch in the chenille ¼ inch (6mm) from the eye.

6 Take the thread to the eye, then wind on the chenille in close turns to create a pronounced head, which mimics a salmon egg. Remove the excess chenille and cast off the thread.

235

Micro Tube

Atlantic salmon

This Micro Tube is tied on ½ inch (1.5cm) of fine-bore plastic tubing, and the technique is the same for virtually all other sizes, including tubes up to 3 inches (7.5cm) long. The tube has no hook at this stage and cannot be fixed in the vise. Instead, it can either be supported on a special tube fly tool, or be pushed over the point of a needle or a "blind" salmon hook that has no eye. Once the tube is secure, the thread and materials are added in the normal way. It is also worth adding a couple of half hitches (single overhand knots) after each process, should the tube inadvertently spin on its support and the thread unwind.

Wing:
Dyed blue squirrel tail and a strand of silver Flashabou

Thread:
Black

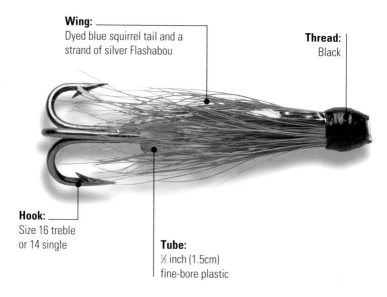

Hook:
Size 16 treble
or 14 single

Tube:
½ inch (1.5cm)
fine-bore plastic

1 Cut a short section of clear plastic tubing and slide it over the point of a specially designed tool for tying tube flies, or over the tapered end of a "blind" salmon hook. Push the tube down so that it fits firmly on the support and doesn't spin around.

2 Run on the tying thread close to the front end of the tube and make about ten turns.

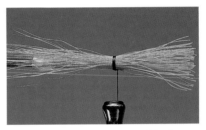

3 Take a small bunch of dyed blue squirrel tail. This type of hair is fine enough for this small fly. Catch the hair in on one side of the tube.

4 Pull the thread tight to fix the hair in place. At the same time allow the hair to flare slightly around the tube so that one half of it is entirely covered.

5 Take a second bunch of hair the same size and color as the first. Twist the tube around on its support and catch this bunch in on the other side so that the hair flares around the tube.

6 Catch in a single strand of silver Flashabou on both sides of the wing. Trim the waste ends of the hair so that the front of the tube is exposed. Build a neat head and cast off with a whip finish.

237

Atlantic
salmon

Willie Gunn

Anglers fishing specifically for Atlantic salmon use Waddington
shanks such as the Willie Gunn for a number of reasons. Like
tube flies, they allow a large fly to be used without the problems
associated with a very thick wire hook or the leverage caused by
a long-shanked hook. These problems are alleviated by a hook
that articulates in a loop to the rear of the Waddington, only the
fly itself having a rigid base. Attaching the hook to a metal loop
also means that, if a hook does become damaged on a rock, it
can easily be replaced, thereby extending the life of the fly.
When attaching a hook to a Waddington, slide a short section of
silicone rubber tubing up the body. Next, open the loop slightly
with a pair of pliers and slip the eye of the hook over the wire
end. Slide the hook into the loop, then squeeze it shut again with
pliers. Finally, slide the tube over the joint between the loop and
the hook eye so that the hook sits in line with the Waddington.

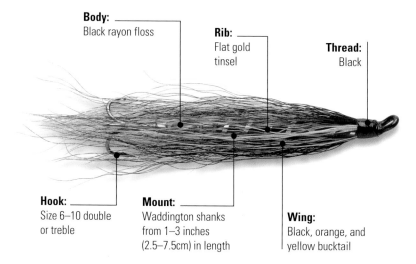

Body:
Black rayon floss

Rib:
Flat gold
tinsel

Thread:
Black

Hook:
Size 6–10 double
or treble

Mount:
Waddington shanks
from 1–3 inches
(2.5–7.5cm) in length

Wing:
Black, orange, and
yellow bucktail

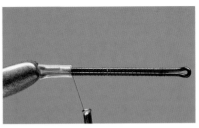

1 Take a short section of silicone tubing and slide it over the hook end of the Waddington shank. Various tube colors can be used—we have used clear here to allow the shank to be seen.

2 Fix the Waddington shank in the vise and push the tube back down as far as it will go. Run on the tying thread at the front loop and carry it in close turns so both lengths of wire are locked together.

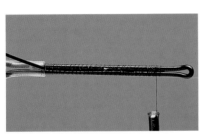

3 At the silicone tubing, catch in 4 inches (10cm) of flat, gold tinsel. Allow the waste end of the tinsel to lie along the shank, then wind the thread over it and up toward the front loop.

4 Catch in a length of black rayon floss. Using the floss on a bobbin holder prevents waste. Carry the floss down the shank in close turns, then back to its catching-in point.

5 Wind the tinsel over the floss body in open, evenly spaced turns. Secure the end and remove the excess tinsel and floss. At the eye, add a mixed bunch of black, orange, and yellow bucktail above and below the shank.

6 Secure the hair in place before building a neat head and casting off the thread. To attach the hook, pull the silicone tubing over the body to leave the loop clear. Open it with pliers, slide on the hook, then pinch it shut again.

239

Fish Identifier

Most fish can be caught on an artificial fly but it is those species belonging to the Salmonidae family that are considered the most sporting of all freshwater fish. There are a large number of species within this family, and here, the most important ones are described. Not all these fish are separate species in their own right—the steelhead and sea trout are sea-run forms of the rainbow and brown trout—but each one is different enough in habit and location to be treated separately.

All the fish covered in this book have a natural range limited to the Northern hemisphere, but some, such as the brown trout, brook trout, and Chinook salmon, have been introduced by man into other regions. The rainbow trout, in particular, has been distributed throughout most of the temperate world. It can now be found as far afield as South America, Europe, South Africa, Australia, and New Zealand, where the water is cool and well oxygenated enough for them to thrive.

Each fish offers a unique challenge, and by altering the tackle and technique used to catch them, the fly-fisher can achieve as much satisfaction from catching a selectively feeding cutthroat, as from battling a much larger salmon.

▶ **Brown Trout** - *Salmo trutta*
Brown trout, although indigenous to Europe, have been introduced into lakes and rivers throughout the world, spread as far as North and South America, Australia, New Zealand, Africa, and India, where they have established self-sustaining populations. Brown trout vary in coloration, ranging from bright silver to olive and

brown to a golden yellow, depending on the habitat in which they are found. In small streams and rivers, they often exhibit the classic brown trout coloration of brown back and butter yellow flanks liberally dotted with black and red spots. In larger lakes, they can range from silver and almost spotless to dark brown and heavily spotted. Although brown trout have been caught on fly well in excess of 20lb (9kg), a fish of 5lb (2.3kg) is considered a specimen.

USE THE FOLLOWING FLIES TO CATCH...

Brown Trout
32 F Fly
34 Elk Hair Emerger
36 Red Tag
38 Polywinged
  Midge
40 Bi-Visible
42 Griffith's Gnat
44 Elk Hair Caddis
46 Adams
48 Light Cahill
50 Royal Wulff
54 Highland Dun
56 Blue-winged
  Olive
58 CDC Dun
60 Parachute Hare's
  Ear
62 Klinkhammer
  Special
64 Daddy Longlegs
66 Gum Beetle
70 Dave's Hopper
72 Balloon Caddis
74 Sparkle Dun
76 Goddard Caddis
78 Turck's
  Tarantula

80 Polywinged
  Spinner
82 Shipman's Buzzer
84 Shuttlecock
86 CDC Emerger
88 Detached Body
  Mayfly
90 Cutwing Caddis
94 Hare's Ear
  Nymph
96 Flashback
  Pheasant Tail
  Nymph
98 Teeny Nymph
100 Red Fox Squirrel
  Nymph
102 Brassie
104 Serendipity
106 Suspender
  Buzzer
108 Egg Fly
110 Rabbit Fly
112 Goldhead Bug
114 Peeping Caddis
116 Sparkle Pupa
118 Timberline
  Emerger
120 Baetis Nymph

122 Woolly Worm
124 Montana
  Nymph
126 Palomino Midge
128 Bloodworm
130 Prince Nymph
132 Scud
134 Czech Nymph
136 Epoxy Nymph
138 Ascending
  Midge Pupa
140 Mudeye
142 Marabou
  Damsel
146 Rubber-legged
  Stonefly Nymph
150 Diawl Bach
152 Soft Hackle
154 Black Pennell
156 Soldier Palmer
158 Bibio
160 Gosling
162 Coachman
164 Blae and Black
166 Silver Butcher
168 Teal, Blue, and
  Silver
170 March Brown

172 Invicta
178 Black Ghost
180 Olive Matuka
184 Viva
186 Appetizer
188 Black Tadpole
190 Woolly Bugger
194 Marabou
  Muddler
196 Muddler
  Minnow
198 Deer-hair Fry
200 Missionary
202 Booby
204 Mrs. Simpson
206 Sparkler
214 Clouser Minnow
216 Thunder Creek
  Silver Shiner
230 Zonker
232 Minkie
234 Egg-sucking
  Leech

241

▼ **Sea Trout** - *Salmo trutta*

This is the sea-run form of the brown trout that spends the majority of its life in estuaries and coastal waters, feeding on a diet of sand eels and shrimps. Though it can be caught in saltwater, it is normally sought in rivers and lakes after it enters freshwater to spawn. In the ocean, it is bright silver with a pale brown back flecked with irregular black spots. After about a week in freshwater, the color darkens considerably. Sea trout grow large, with fish well into double figures often caught. In Patagonia and Tierra del Fuego, specimens over 30lb (13.5kg) have been taken on artificial fly.

▼ **Rainbow Trout** - *Oncorhynchus mykiss*

The rainbow trout's original range extends along the U.S.'s Pacific coast from Alaska to California through to Northeast Asia. Man's intervention in the quest to provide sport fishing in other parts of the world has seen the species being introduced to most of the Earth's temperate regions. There are a variety of strains, including those from the Shasta and Kamloops, though the bulk of rainbow trout in many stocked waters have a mixed ancestry. Some even exhibit the orange flash of the cutthroat, resulting from the fact that the two species readily hybridize. The rainbow trout's coloration varies widely, from a dark, heavily spotted form with a green back and a bright pink stripe running the length of the body to a silver, almost spotless one. Rainbow trout are found in both rivers and lakes feeding on a variety of prey from small invertebrates to fish and even small mammals.

USE THE FOLLOWING FLIES TO CATCH...

Sea Trout
64 Daddy Longlegs
40 Bi-Visible
94 Hare's Ear
 Nymph
104 Serendipity
154 Black Pennell
156 Soldier Palmer
158 Bibio
162 Coachman
166 Silver Butcher
168 Teal, Blue, and
 Silver
222 Stoat's Tail

Rainbow Trout
32 F Fly
34 Elk Hair
 Emerger
36 Red Tag
38 Polywinged
 Midge
40 Bi-Visible
42 Griffith's Gnat
44 Elk Hair Caddis
46 Adams
48 Light Cahill
50 Royal Wulff
52 Humpy
54 Highland Dun
56 Blue-winged
 Olive
58 CDC Dun

60 Parachute Hare's
 Ear
62 Klinkhammer
 Special
64 Daddy Longlegs
66 Gum Beetle
68 Stimulator
70 Dave's Hopper
72 Balloon Caddis
74 Sparkle Dun
76 Goddard Caddis
78 Turck's Tarantula
80 Polywinged
 Spinner
82 Shipman's Buzzer
84 Shuttlecock
86 CDC Emerger
88 Detached Body
 Mayfly
90 Cutwing Caddis
94 Hare's Ear
 Nymph
96 Flashback
 Pheasant Tail
 Nymph
98 Teeny Nymph
100 Red Fox Squirrel
 Nymph
102 Brassie
104 Serendipity
106 Suspender
 Buzzer
108 Egg Fly

110 Rabbit Fly
112 Goldhead Bug
114 Peeping
 Caddis
116 Sparkle Pupa
118 Timberline
 Emerger
120 Baetis Nymph
122 Woolly Worm
124 Montana
 Nymph
126 Palomino
 Nymph
128 Bloodworm
130 Prince Nymph
132 Scud
134 Czech Nymph
136 Epoxy Buzzer
138 Ascending
 Midge Pupa
140 Mudeye
142 Marabou
 Damsel
146 Rubber-legged
 Stonefly Nymph
150 Diawl Bach
152 Soft Hackle
154 Black Pennell
156 Soldier Palmer
158 Bibio
162 Coachman
164 Blae and Black
166 Silver Butcher

168 Teal, Blue, and
 Silver
170 March Brown
172 Invicta
178 Black Ghost
180 Olive Matuka
184 Viva
186 Appetizer
188 Black Tadpole
190 Woolly Bugger
194 Marabou
 Minnow
196 Muddler
 Minnow
198 Deer-hair Fry
200 Missionary
202 Booby
204 Mrs. Simpson
206 Sparkler
210 Mickey Finn
214 Clouser Minnow
216 Thunder Creek
 Silver Shiner
230 Zonker
232 Minkie
234 Egg-sucking
 Leech

► **Steelhead** -

Oncorhynchus mykiss

The steelhead is the sea-run form of the rainbow trout and a highly sought-after species. It can be caught as it enters its spawning rivers on a range of fly patterns, from bucktails and streamers to dry flies. Fresh in from the ocean, the steelhead is in prime condition. It has a dark bluish-gray back and silver flanks, and the upper half of its body is

USE THE FOLLOWING FLIES TO CATCH...

Steelhead
50 Royal Wulff
52 Humpy
68 Stimulator
76 Goddard Caddis
98 Teeny Nymph
108 Egg Fly
182 Alaskabou
192 Babine Special
196 Muddler
   Minnow
212 Polar Shrimp

Cutthroat
32 F Fly
38 Polywinged
   Midge
42 Griffith's Gnat
44 Elk Hair Caddis
46 Adams
48 Light Cahill
50 Royal Wulff
52 Humpy
56 Blue-winged
   Olive
58 CDC Dun
60 Parachute Hare's
   Ear
68 Stimulator
70 Dave's Hopper
72 Balloon Caddis
74 Sparkle Dun
76 Goddard Caddis
78 Turck's Tarantula
80 Polywinged
   Spinner
86 CDC Emerger
88 Detached Body
   Mayfly
90 Cutwing Caddis
94 Hare's Ear
   Nymph
96 Flashback
   Pheasant Tail
   Nymph
100 Red Fox Squirrel
   Nymph
102 Brassie
104 Serendipity
108 Egg Fly
112 Goldhead Bug
114 Peeping Caddis
118 Timberland
   Emerger
120 Baetis Nymph
122 Woolly Worm
124 Montana
   Nymph
132 Scud
146 Rubber-legged
   Stonefly Nymph
178 Black Ghost
180 Olive Matuka
190 Woolly Bugger
194 Marabou
   Muddler
196 Muddler
   Minnow
210 Mickey Finn
216 Thunder Creek
   Silver Shiner

Arctic Char
32 F Fly
38 Polywinged
   Midge
42 Griffith's Gnat
46 Adams
50 Royal Wulff
74 Sparkle Dun
86 CDC Emerger
104 Serendipity
108 Egg Fly
112 Goldhead Bug
178 Black Ghost
190 Woolly Bugger
192 Babine Special
194 Marabou
   Minnow
196 Muddler
   Minnow
210 Mickey Finn
216 Thunder Creek
   Silver Shiner
230 Zonker
234 Egg-sucking
   Leech

covered in small black spots. However, after a few days in the river, it begins to darken into its spawning colors. Steelhead grow large and while a 10lb (4.5kg) fish is a specimen, it has been caught on a fly weighing in excess of 30lb (13.5kg).

▶ **Cutthroat** - *Oncorhynchus clarki*

Closely related to the rainbow trout and the various species of Pacific salmon, the cutthroat gets its name from the distinctive red mark under its throat. It is found in a variety of habitats in both rivers and lakes and also has a migratory form that spends part of its life in the ocean. The coloration of the cutthroat is extremely variable, and there are a number of subspecies, however, the basic color is olive with golden sides liberally covered in tiny black spots, particularly along the back and toward the tail. Cutthroat can be caught on a variety of fly patterns, from tiny spinner and dun imitations, for the fish of clear, shallow creeks, to large streamers and dry flies when fishing lakes and big rivers.

◀ **Arctic Char -**
Salvelinus alpinus
As they reach spawning condition, Arctic char take on a superb coloration. The males become bright orange in the flanks contrasted with a dark olive to black back. The pectoral, pelvic,

245

and anal fins also turn bright orange, edged with pure white that is extremely visible in clear water. Although often encountered as the sea-run form below latitude 64 degrees, the Arctic char is normally found landlocked in lakes. These populations rarely grow as large as the sea-run fish.

Other char species include the brook trout, *Salvelinus fontinalis*, the lake trout, *Salvelinus namaycush*, and the dolly varden, *Salvelinus malma*. The brook trout is sometimes known as the speckled char, and needs cold, high quality water if it is to thrive. The dolly varden is found in North America and eastern Asia, and is similar in form to the Arctic char. The back is steel blue and the silvery belly is liberally spotted with cream and pink. The lake trout is the largest of the char species, growing in excess of 100lb (45.4kg). Normally found in very deep water, it can be caught on fly in shallow water when targeting grayling, which are its main prey.

▶ **Grayling** -
Thymallus arcticus
/Thymallus thymallus
There are two main
species of grayling. *Thymallus arcticus* is
found in the northern U.S., Canada, and
northeast Asia, where it mainly inhabits rivers. *Thymallus thymallus* is the European species that exists from the U.K. in the west to the Black Sea in the east. It is also found throughout Scandinavia. Both species are quite similar, with an olive-gray body and a silvery-gray belly over which there are a few, small, black spots. The main difference between the two is the size of

the colorful dorsal fin. In the European species, it is large, but in T. *arcticus*, it is enormous, especially in the males. This fin is used to great effect when the fish is hooked and helps it kite across the current.

Grayling are normally caught on small dry flies and nymphs, though the larger specimens are known to feed on small mammals and can be taken on very large dry flies.

▶ **Coho Salmon** - *Oncorhynchus kisutch*

Coho, or silver salmon as they are usually known, are great sporting fish, especially when fished for with light tackle. Fresh in from the ocean, their flanks are a burnished silver and at this stage they are ready takers of the fly. One of the Pacific salmon species, the coho's natural range includes the waters of the northern U.S. and Canada to northeast Asia. It has also been

USE THE FOLLOWING FLIES TO CATCH...

Grayling			Coho Salmon
32 F Fly	60 Parachute Hare's	104 Serendipity	52 Humpy
36 Red Tag	Ear	108 Egg Fly	68 Stimulator
38 Polywinged	62 Klinkhammer	112 Goldhead Bug	98 Teeny Nymph
Midge	Special	114 Peeping Caddis	108 Egg Fly
42 Griffith's Gnat	72 Balloon Caddis	116 Sparkle Pupa	212 Polar Shrimp
44 Elk Hair	74 Sparkle Dun	120 Baetis Nymph	230 Zonker
Caddis	86 CDC Emerger	132 Scud	234 Egg-sucking
46 Adams	94 Hare's Ear	134 Czech Nymph	Leech
48 Light Cahill	Nymph	152 Soft Hackle	
56 Blue-winged	96 Flashback	162 Coachman	
Olive	Pheasant Tail	192 Babine Special	
58 CDC Dun	Nymph		
	102 Brassie		

247

introduced into the Great Lakes of Canada and the northeast side of the United States. A hard fighting fish, the silver can always be differentiated from the chinook by the fact that it has white rather than black gums. Like all salmon, once it has entered its spawning river, the silver coloration fades, and in the coho's case is replaced by a dark, grayish back, reddish flanks, and a grayish-green head.

▼ **Atlantic Salmon** - *Salmo salar*
The range of the Atlantic salmon is from Russia in the east through Scandinavia, the U.K., and Ireland across the Atlantic to the eastern coast of Canada and the U.S. Fresh in from the sea it has a dark gray back and silver flanks, often with a slight lilac hue. A river running in spate after heavy rain is the trigger for the salmon to run into their spawning rivers. For the first few days in freshwater, Atlantic salmon are ready takers of the fly, but the longer they spend in the river, the darker and less easy to catch they become. Unlike the Pacific salmon species, *Salmo salar* doesn't always die after spawning. This means that some fish

USE THE FOLLOWING FLIES TO CATCH...

Atlantic Salmon	160 Gosling	228 Ally's Shrimp	Chinook Salmon
40 Bi-Visible	174 Curry's Red	236 Micro Tube	98 Teeny Nymph
52 Humpy	Shrimp	238 Willie Gunn	182 Alaskabou
76 Goddard Caddis	218 The Garry		192 Babine Special
104 Serendipity	220 Munro Killer		230 Zonker
108 Egg Fly	222 Stoat's Tail		234 Egg-sucking
154 Black Pennell	224 Blue Charm		Leech
158 Bibio	226 Silver Rat		

manage to migrate back into the ocean to return in subsequent years, having grown fat again on a diet of small fish and crustaceans. In many rivers, there are four distinct runs. The first are the spring fish that are often large and in excess of 20lb (9kg). The next run comes in early summer, followed by a run of small single sea-winter fish known as grilse. The final run comes in the fall just prior to actual spawning and includes many of the largest specimens, which in some river systems can include fish of over 50lb (22.7kg).

▼ **Chinook Salmon** - *Oncorhynchus tshawytscha*
The chinook, or king salmon, is the largest of all the Pacific salmon species, attaining weights of well over 100lb (45.4kg). Fish of this size, however, are rarely caught by anglers, and for the fly-fisher specimens of 50lb (22.7kg) or so are considered a real trophy. The chinook's range includes the west coast of the northern U.S. and Canada across to northeast Asia. Being such a highly sought-after species, it has also been introduced into other parts of the world, most notably South America and southern Australia. Of all the Pacific salmon, the king is the one that changes into its spawning garb the quickest, and while bright silver "chromers" are caught, when in freshwater the majority have already taken on the typical maroon-colored flanks of a fish in breeding condition. Although normally differentiated from the coho salmon by its much larger size, the fact that the king has black rather than white gums makes identification easy.

249

Degree of difficulty

The flies in this book are rated on a scale of 1 to 5 according to the difficulty involved in tying them. Flies with one icon are the simplest to tie, and flies with five icons the most complex. This chart lists them in order of difficulty:

⌛

32 F Fly
42 Griffith's Gnat
102 Brassie
126 Palomino
    Midge

⌛⌛

36 Red Tag
38 Polywinged
    Midge
66 Gum Beetle
72 Balloon Caddis
82 Shipman's
    Buzzer
84 Shuttlecock
94 Hare's Ear
    Nymph
98 Teeny Nymph
106 Suspender
    Buzzer
108 Egg Fly
112 Goldhead Bug
128 Bloodworm
150 Diawl Bach
152 Soft Hackle
156 Soldier
    Palmer

⌛⌛⌛

44 Elk Hair Caddis
46 Adams
68 Stimulator
74 Sparkle Dun

76 Goddard Caddis
80 Polywinged
    Spinner
86 CDC Emerger
100 Red Fox
    Squirrel Nymph
110 Rabbit Fly
114 Peeping Caddis
118 Timberline
    Emerger
122 Woolly Worm
124 Montana
    Nymph
130 Prince Nymph
132 Scud
134 Czech Nymph
136 Epoxy Buzzer
154 Black Pennell
158 Bibio
162 Coachman
180 Olive Matuka
182 Alaskabou
184 Viva
186 Appetizer
188 Black Tadpole
190 Woolly Bugger
192 Babine Special
200 Missionary
202 Booby
206 Sparkler
210 Mickey Finn
212 Polar Shrimp
214 Clouser
    Minnow
218 The Garry
220 Munro Killer

222 Stoat's Tail
224 Blue Charm
230 Zonker
232 Minkie
234 Egg-sucking
    Leech
236 Micro Tube
238 Willie Gun

⌛⌛⌛⌛

34 Elk Hair Emerger
40 Bi-Visible
48 Light Cahill
50 Royal Wulff
52 Humpy
54 Highland Dun
56 Blue-winged
    Olive
58 CDC Dun
60 Parachute
    Hare's Ear
62 Klinkhammer
    Special
64 Daddy Longlegs
78 Turck's
    Tarantula
88 Detached Body
    Mayfly
90 Cutwing Caddis
96 Flashback
    Pheasant Tail
    Nymph
104 Serendipity
116 Sparkle Pupa
120 Baetis Nymph

142 Marabou
    Damsel
146 Rubber-legged
    Stonefly Nymph
160 Gosling
164 Blae and Black
166 Silver Butcher
168 Teal, Blue, and
    Silver
170 March Brown
172 Invicta
178 Black Ghost
194 Marabou
    Muddler
196 Muddler
    Minnow
204 Mrs Simpson
216 Thunder Creek
    Silver Shiner
226 Silver Rat
228 Ally's Shrimp

⌛⌛⌛⌛⌛

70 Dave's Hopper
138 Ascending
    Midge Pupa
140 Mudeye
174 Curry's Red
    Shrimp
198 Deer-hair Fry

Glossary

Buzzer A term used by anglers for the chironomid midge in its various stages. The name comes from the fact that the swarming adults create a loud buzzing sound.

Chenille A soft, fluffy material that is spun on a central core. Great for tying chunky bodies on streamers and hairwings. The name comes from the French word for caterpillar.

Chironomid midge A small aquatic insect that is found in vast numbers in rivers and lakes throughout the world. The larvae, pupae, and adults form a large part of the trout's diet.

Dapping A technique for fishing an artificial fly without a fly line. Instead a long rod and a short length of air-resistant blow-line are used allowing the fly to be drifted out over the water.

Dave Shipman A top British trout angler responsible for a number of effective trout patterns including the Shipman's Buzzer.

Emerger A term used to describe an artificial fly tied to imitate an aquatic insect at the very point when it emerges from its pupal skin.

Hans Van Klinken A Dutch fly-tyer responsible for a number of modern patterns, most notably the Klinkhammer Special.

Lead eyes Dumbbell shaped weights tied in at the eye of the hook prior to adding the rest of the materials. They help the fly to sink quickly and can be painted to resemble the eyes of a fish.

Loch style A method of fishing where the angler casts over the side of a boat drifting with the wind. Used primarily on large lakes typically in Scotland and Ireland.

Mayfly A large group of aquatic insects with upright wings. Ranging in size from $\frac{1}{8}$ in (3mm) to more than $1\frac{1}{2}$ in (4cm) in length, the various species make up a large part of the diet of both trout and grayling.

Mottled marabou Rather than using the plain white domestic variety of turkey, the feathers of the wild form are dyed to provide a mottled effect. Great for tying all kinds of nymph patterns.

Roman Moser A top Austrian fly fisher who has created a range of simple but effective fly patterns, most notably the Balloon Caddis.

Spider A simple form of wet fly comprising just a body and a sparse collar hackle. It is not actually tied to imitate a spider, but rather a nymph or emerging adult insect.

Tube fly A fly tied on a section of tube rather than a hook. The tube itself is used in a range of lengths and can be formed from various materials depending on the sink rate required. These include plastic, aluminum, and brass.

Vernille A form of chenille where the fibers are stuck rather than spun on to the central core. Tougher than ordinary chenille, in the finer diameters it can be used to make detached bodies.

251

Suppliers list

North America

Badger Creek Fly Tying
622 West Dryden Road
Freeville, NY 13068
USA
Tel: (607) 347 4946
www.mwflytying.com

The Bearlodge Angler
612 Grace Avenue
Worland, WY 82401
USA
Tel: (307) 347 4002
Fax: (307) 347 3371
www.w3trib.com/~kmorris

Dan Bailey's Fly Shop
209 West Park Street
PO Box 1019
Livingston, MT 59047
USA
Tel: (406) 222 1673
Fax: (406) 222 8450
www.dan-bailey.com

FishUSA.com
2315 West Grandview Blvd.
Erie, PA 16506
USA
Tel: (814) 835 3600
Fax: (814) 835 3671
www.fishusa.com

Knoll's Yellowstone Hackle
104 Chicory (Fishing Access) Road
Pray, MT 59065
USA
Tel: (406) 333 4848
www.avicom.net/knoll

Lowe Fly Shop
15 Woodland Drive
Waynesville, NC 28786
USA
Tel: (828) 452 0039
www.loweflyshop.com

North American Angler
211 Moore Dr
Hanover, PA 17331, USA
Tel: (888) 420 0404
www.northamericanangler.com

The Orvis Company
1711 Blue Hills Drive
Roanoke, VA 24012, USA
Tel: (540) 345 4606
Fax: (540) 343 7053
www.orvis.com

Rocky Mountain Flies
PO Box 76114
Edmonton, Alberta
Canada T6H 5Y7
Tel/Fax: (780) 439 6453
www.rockymountainflies.com

RoundRocks Fly Fishing
PO Box 4059
Logan, UT 84323, USA
Tel: (800) 992-8774
www.roundrocks.com

UNI Products J.G. Côté Inc
561 Principale
Ste-Mélanie, QC
Canada J0K 3A0
Tel: (450) 889 2195
Fax: (450) 889 8506
www.uniproducts.com

UK

Ellis Slater
47 Bridge Cross Road
Chase Terrace
Burntwood
WS7 8BU, UK
Tel: (01543) 671377

Farlows
5 Pall Mall
London
SW1Y 5NP, UK
Tel: (020) 7839 2423
Fax: (020) 7839 8959
www.farlows.co.uk

Lyttle's of Dunchurch
2 Southam Road
Dunchurch
Warwickshire
CV22 6NL, UK
Tel: (01788) 817044

Sportfish
Winforton
Hereford
HR3 6EB, UK
Tel: (01544) 327 111
Fax: (01544) 327 093
www.sportfish.co.uk

Tom C Saville Ltd
9 Nottingham Road
Trowell
Nottingham
NG9 3PA, UK
Tel: (0115) 930 8800
Fax: (0115) 930 3336

Australia and New Zealand

BCS Enterprises Ltd
PO Box 30361
Lower Hutt
New Zealand
Tel: (64) 4589 3302
www.bcsent.co.nz

The Flyshop
RMB 1270 Goulburn Valley Hwy
Thornton
Vic. 3712, Australia
Tel: (1800) 458 111
Fax: (03) 5773 2514
www.theflyshop.com.au

Flyworld
Anglers International
PO Box 167
Bayswater
WA 6933, Australia
Tel: (08) 9375 8228
www.flyworld.com.au

Pro Tackle
284 Ross River Rd
Townsville
NQ 4814, Australia
Tel: (07) 4775 7677
Fax: (07) 4728 7525
www.protackle.com.au

Tackle Tactics
PO Box 53
Foxton
New Zealand
Tel: 06 363 5957
Fax: 06 363 5958
www.tackletactics.co.nz

Index

Credits

Quarto would like to thank and acknowledge the following for supplying pictures used in this book:

Peter Gathercole page 7 and 10

All other photographs and illustrations are the copyright of Quarto Publishing plc. While every effort has been made to credit contributors, Quarto would like to apologize should there have been any ommissions or errors.